To Elmer Schwartz —
who helped make and
shares our Cleveland history.
With all good wishes,

Sidney Vincent
Judah Rubinstein

Merging Traditions — Jewish Life in Cleveland

MERGING TRADITIONS —

JEWISH LIFE IN CLEVELAND

A Contemporary Narrative 1945–1975
A Pictorial Record 1839–1975

by
Sidney Z. Vincent
and
Judah Rubinstein

A JOINT PUBLICATION
The Western Reserve Historical Society
The Jewish Community Federation of Cleveland

Library of Congress Cataloging in Publication Data

Vincent, Sidney Z
    Merging traditions.

    (Western Reserve Historical Society publication ; no. 144)
    Includes bibliographical references.
    1. Jews in Cleveland—History—20th century. 2. Jews in
Cleveland—Pictorial works. 3. Cleveland—History—20th cen-
tury. 4. Cleveland—Description—Views. I. Rubinstein, Judah,
joint author. II. Title. III. Series: Western Reserve Historical
Society, Cleveland. Publication ; no. 144.
F499.C69J548   977.1'32'004924   78-10307
ISBN 0-911704-18-3

This publication
is made possible
through a fund established
by the generosity of
the children and friends
of
Mollie and Max Simon
and
the following community leaders
who have served as Presidents of the
Jewish Community Federation:
Leo W. Neumark, 1959–1962
Myron E. Glass, 1962–1965
David N. Myers, 1965–1968
Lloyd S. Schwenger, 1968–1971
Maurice Saltzman, 1971–1974
Morton L. Mandel, 1974–1977
Albert B. Ratner, 1977–

Preface

In recent years the photograph has come to be recognized as more than a curiosity or a device to stimulate antiquarian instincts. In addition to serving useful artistic and sentimental purposes, the photograph can be as important a literal record as the written word. In this book, both the photograph and written word have been joined to present in a scholarly, if not academic, way a statement on the history of the Cleveland Jewish community.

While the competence and ability of both Sidney Z. Vincent and Judah Rubinstein will be evident to those who read the narrative and study the photographs, we would like to add a word of appreciation to both. Each gave much time and thought and energy to this work. Writing of the recent past is no easy task, nor is searching for and identifying and evaluating photographs which reposed with families and institutions throughout the community.

We would also like to acknowledge with thanks the individuals and institutions that either deposited original photographs with the Cleveland Jewish Archives at the Historical Society or allowed copies of their heirlooms to be made. The community has been very responsive to our appeals for records of this type.

Kermit J. Pike
Director of the Library

The Western Reserve Historical Society is pleased to join with the Jewish Community Federation of Cleveland in presenting this book. We trust that it will serve both to please and to instruct.

THE WESTERN RESERVE HISTORICAL SOCIETY
Frederick C. Crawford, Chairman of the Board
Robert C. McDowell, President
Meredith B. Colket, Jr., Executive Director

Foreword

THE origins of this book go back to 1954 when the nationwide celebration of the tercentenary of the first Jewish settlement in America caused many communities to record and preserve their own history.

In Cleveland, the Jewish Community Federation commissioned the American Jewish History Center of the Jewish Theological Seminary to write the history of the Cleveland Jewish community from its beginning in 1837 to 1945. The cut-off date was chosen because it represented a major watershed in Jewish history, the ending of the Second World War. However, when the draft of that volume by Professor Lloyd Gartner of Tel Aviv University was completed, there was a unanimous feeling that the story could not end there. The decades since 1945, by general agreement, were considered the most dynamic period in American Jewish history, since they saw a maturation of Jewish communal life throughout the United States, not least in Cleveland.

These were the years when the Jewish community lived through the tragedy and the triumph of the two most decisive events of Jewish history in millennia—the Holocaust and the establishment of the State of Israel. No Jew, no Jewish community anywhere, was unaffected by these cataclysmic, monumental events. Our lives as Jews would never again be the same.

And these were decisive years in domestic as well as overseas events. The Jewish community played a leading role in the civil rights movement. The alienation of youth from tradition in general affected our community pro-

foundly, as part of the revolt against "establishments" of all kinds. The astonishing mobility of our people resulted in changing neighborhoods, inevitably generating major problems. The virtual end of immigration and the rise of a native–born generation created a basic challenge to all our institutions to deepen their Jewish content in order to meet the increased threat of assimilation.

How did the Jewish community of Cleveland respond to these crises—the dangers, the challenges, and the opportunities of our time? The answer begged to be recorded both for its own sake and for the sake of future generations.

As the following pages reveal, Cleveland was intimately involved in all these and many other problems, emerging in the postwar period as certainly one of the leading Jewish communities in the country. The record of that leadership is the story of this volume. The authors, Sidney Z. Vincent and Judah Rubinstein, make no claim to writing a history in the strict academic sense of that term. It was not possible, for example, to include many major actors in that thirty-year drama. They have described their volume as an impressionistic account—through narrative, for which Sidney Vincent is responsible, and photographs, for which Judah Rubinstein is responsible—of this community's development and growth. Both have served for decades professionally in Jewish communal work as members of the staff of the Jewish Community Federation and therefore bring to this volume the intimacy and perhaps the particularized point of view of those who have not only observed but have participated in the history-making. Richard E. Karberg, photographic associate, added much to this effort by his extensive knowledge of urban life and pictorial sources. His talent as a photographer enriches the extensive photo-documentary sections of this volume.

The Jewish Community Federation expresses its deep thanks to Miriam Klein, Dan Simon, and Chialeen Stern, the children of the beloved Max Simon, the only member of our community to serve as President of both the Jewish Community Council and the Jewish Community Federation. Through a fund established in memory of their parents, they have underwritten the major cost of the publication of the volume. Appreciation is also due to seven presidents of the Federation who agreed to underwrite the balance to ensure publication.

Finally, the Federation is gratified that the Western Reserve Historical Society joined us as co-publishers. The result has been a most felicitous relationship, during which the Society has been highly cooperative in every detail of the undertaking, constantly demonstrating its enthusiasm for this publication. Two members of its staff, John Grabowski, ethnic archives specialist, and Sandra Berman, archivist of the Cleveland Jewish Archives, were constantly helpful throughout the months of research on this project.

Our special thanks are due to Howard Allen, our book consultant, who guided this volume through its many stages of preparation to publication.

It is our hope that the readers of this volume will derive enlightenment and pleasure from it, particularly since so many of them helped to create the history which it records.

The Cleveland Jewish History Committee
Irving Kane, Chairman
Eugene H. Freedheim
Frank E. Joseph
David N. Myers
Ben D. Zevin

Contents

I

A Contemporary
Narrative
1945–1975

External Relationships

WHEN Japan surrendered in August, 1945, there were two days of celebration. Banks and stores closed, there was dancing in the streets, special programs were broadcast on the radio, and prayer meetings of thanksgiving were held in churches and synagogues. But even before the celebration ended, the question of "What now?" arose more and more insistently, nowhere more than in the Jewish community. The Second World War was a watershed for everybody, but the old witticism about Jews being like everybody else, only more so, never seemed more apt. The changes that were to engulf America—racial, sexual, technological, economic, transforming the basic fabric of American society—would strike with particular immediacy at the Jewish community, which was only beginning fully to grasp the horrors of the Hitler era. Cleveland was to play a leading role in the drama about to unfold.

For a generation, the centers of Jewish population had been in the East 105th Street district and the Kinsman area. A gradual but increasing spill into the Heights had begun after the First World War, and by 1944 it had reached such proportions that barely more than half the Jewish population still lived in Cleveland proper, almost all within the two districts mentioned.

Within a decade fewer than one in ten Jews remained in the city proper, and by 1960 the migration had gone so far that a chapter on the Cleveland Jewish community in the book, *A Tale of Ten Cities*, was entitled, "Cleveland, City without Jews."[1] It made the claim that not a single Jewish child that year would graduate from a Cleveland high school. Almost every American city would soon experience the same dramatic outward thrust, but it happened first, most dramatically, and most completely in Cleveland.

With only two exceptions, Mt. Sinai Hospital and the Jewish Community Federation, every Jewish organization moved out of Cleveland proper in the postwar period. (The Temple retained its historic building on East 105th Street, which was declared a national historic landmark, but many of its major activities were transferred to its suburban branch.) The eastward pull was so strong that by 1970 the problem of changing neighborhoods again became a central issue; this time the question was whether the Jewish neighborhoods in the inner suburbs, particularly Cleveland Heights, could survive.

Nor was the shift in population limited to movements within Cuyahoga County. One universal effect of the war was to expose thousands of young men to the South, Southwest, and Far West, where the vast majority of military training camps were located. Many of them were attracted by the more pleasant weather and freer life styles they found there or by the hope of greater economic opportunities, and the trickle of emigration to the West and South which had started at the close of the First World War swelled to a flood. The observance of the fiftieth anniversary of the founding of Camp Wise, in 1957, was celebrated in Los Angeles as well as in Cleveland, so numerous were the "alumni" of that institution; Cleveland Clubs sprang up in California, reminiscent of the *lands-*

4 *manshaften* established earlier in the century; obituary notices in Cleveland papers frequently noted survivors now living in Arizona and Florida and California.

There was nothing in the population figures to indicate that a community so mobile and so certain to lose a significant proportion of its restless youth to more attractive sections of the country would nevertheless emerge at the end of the next generation of experience (from 1945 to 1975) as one of the most creative and productive Jewish communities on the continent. Nor did the status of the city itself, so crucial to the development of the Jewish community, warrant a prediction of optimism in 1945. Among American cities Cleveland was then sixth in population; by 1975 it was twelfth, with predictions that it would be seventeenth by 1980, the second highest percentage loss of the fifty largest cities of the country.[2]

The decline in population was symptomatic of a malaise that ran deep. As the postwar period drew to a close, every industrial city in the Midwest was suffering from growing competition with warmer areas of the country belatedly moving into the industrial age. But nowhere was the pressure felt more strongly than in Cleveland, the center of a heavy industry in danger of growing obsolete, with a decaying downtown, uninspired political leadership, and a growing racial polarity that divided the city into a predominantly white West Side and a predominantly black East Side.

And yet, against these odds, the Jewish community of Greater Cleveland blossomed during the three decades in a way that gave much Jewish validity to the official civic boast: "Cleveland: The Best Location in the Nation." At one time in the sixties eight Clevelanders were simultaneously presidents of major national and international Jewish organizations;[3] of the ten largest federations in the country, eight were headed by professional directors who were Cleveland-trained (most of them also Cleveland-born),[4] a spectacular contribution by a community comprising about one and a half percent of the national Jewish population. So prolific was that massive representation of Clevelanders in national organizations and so prominent was their participation in national discussions and decisions that good-humored but wry references to "the Cleveland Mafia" were common. And while Cleveland Jews occasionally complained that they were constantly called upon to assume more than their fair share of responsibility for various philanthropic enterprises because so much was expected of them, they nevertheless took pride in a community that was traditionally "Number One" in responding to human needs.

In areas of community activity where it was possible to measure results with some precision, the Cleveland record was outstanding. Beginning in 1948, in per capita giving to the United Jewish Appeal, Cleveland was first or occasionally second every year among the large cities of the country. Over the thirty-year period it was easily the most generous, with only Detroit a serious competitor. Its support of national Jewish organizations was also outstanding. In a 1974 Council of Jewish Federations report Cleveland ranked either first or second among the sixteen major Jewish communities in its support of national community relations and cultural service agencies. Its network of service agencies (the Jewish Family Service Association, Bellefaire, two homes for the aged, the Jewish Community Center, Mt. Sinai Hospital, the Jewish Vocational Service, the educational agencies) were known throughout the country for high standards of performance. The Jewish Community Federation of Cleveland was the only federation to win

1. Coventry Road, Cleveland Heights. ca. 1926 (Fraser Realty Company)

2. Ark, Heights Jewish Center, Cleveland Heights. 1975 (Richard E. Karberg)

3. B'nai Jeshurun, Temple on the Heights; dedicated 1925; architect Charles R. Greco. 1977 (Steve Stregevsky)

6 the Shroder Award of the Council of Jewish Federations (CJF), awarded for excellence of projects undertaken, three times.

How to explain this contradiction between the somber facts of economics and demography on the one hand, and the achievement of a kind of Golden Age of communal performance on the other? This chapter supplies no definitive answer to that question, which in any case probably defies precise explanation. It does, however, undertake to describe the mix of leadership and activities and projects and issues that made up that thirty-year history, in the hope that such a review will supply some of the human data basic to any evaluation of the history of the Cleveland Jewish community.

Jewish Cleveland in 1945

East 105th Street in 1945 was still the living heart of the Jewish community, as it had been since 1920. The yellow street cars that rumbled north along the tracks in that narrow street, always clogged with traffic, entered the general area of Jewish activity as soon as they crossed Euclid Avenue, Cleveland's main thoroughfare. First, they passed The Temple, majestic and imposing, crowded every Sunday morning with Jew and non-Jew alike, there to hear Rabbi Abba Hillel Silver's weekly sermon; then Mt. Sinai Hospital, soon to become one of the major medical centers of the city; then down the hill, with Rockefeller lagoon and its rowboats and the tennis courts, prime recreation centers for Jewish youth, to the left, and, to the right, the old mansion the Bureau of Jewish Education had bought to be its first permanent headquarters. Then up the grade again, past the Wade Park district with its fine homes, a modest percentage still owned by Jews though the process of moving to the Heights was already well advanced.

But it was only north of Superior Avenue that the Jewish neighborhood really came into its own. Almost every block from Superior to St. Clair had its own *shul* and its own kosher meat market—and fruit and vegetable markets, drug stores, creameries, bakeries, and grocery stores abounded. All of them were meeting places where Jewish events were discussed and where the shape of the day and the week was permeated with the rhythm of Jewish life, reflected not only in the almost total closing down of business on the Jewish holidays, but also in the shared experiences of shopping and dating and discussing in an atmosphere that took Jewish concerns and *Yiddishkeit* for granted.
At class reunions nostalgic memories are still traded—of waiting for "my next" on Saturday night at the jammed meat market, or buying corned beef at Solomon's on Massie Avenue, or smelling the newly baked rye and pumpernickel in any of the bakeries clustered around Earle and Gooding Avenues.

The two major anchor points of the neighborhood were the Jewish Center (later to be known as Park Synagogue) on the corner of Grantwood Avenue, and Glenville High School on Parkwood Drive and Englewood Avenue.

No institution in Cleveland Jewish history, before or since, had so galvanizing an influence on a neighborhood as the Jewish Center. It was for over two decades far more than just a synagogue. Its swimming pool and handball courts and basketball floor were unmatched (the Council Educational Alliance, on Kinsman, had only a small basketball court and none of the other facilities); its auditorium not only hosted the usual dances and lectures for its own members, but also served the entire 105th Street neighborhood, which had no other comparable facility; its classrooms housed the Cleveland Hebrew Schools at a time when that institution was

Montefiore Home, Cleveland Heights; architect Charles R. Greco; dedicated 1921. (Montefiore Home)

most thriving. And throughout the twenties there was the towering figure of Rabbi Solomon Goldman, whose charisma extended far beyond the Jewish Center. Old timers still talk about his lively discussion groups on basic Jewish and human issues involving young talent from every part of the city.[5] Other congregations were dynamic and effective during the period but lacked either the location or the facilities to serve a comparable neighborhood function. Of the three largest, the Euclid Avenue Temple was miles away from its own constituency, The Temple had been built in the university and park district, which had no surrounding Jewish neighborhood, and the Temple on the Heights was ahead of its time, in a neighborhood that had not yet attained its full Jewish growth.

Glenville High School achieved the central position in the Jewish community occupied a generation earlier by Central High and a generation later by Cleveland Heights High, but to a far greater degree. In 1945 the school was still more than seventy percent Jewish and had developed a cohesiveness and pride in its student body reflected years later in an astonishing number of class reunions. These typically featured talk about how high school had more lasting effects upon life patterns than the subsequent college experience. In moments of high rhetoric and accompanying sentimentality, the impact of the three years at Glenville, with its pathetic football teams and its extraordinarily high standards of scholarship, was likened to that of "the playing fields of Eton" upon a generation of Englishmen.

Both institutions, the Jewish Center and Glenville High, derived their Jewish vitality primarily from the intense concentration of the Jewish population. The entire neighborhood encompassed not much more than a single square mile, but it contained a substantial proportion of the total Jewish population and more than half its institutions. Evidently a kind of critical mass was produced, forging a unity that held firm when the outward movement began in earnest and probably accounting for an almost unique Cleveland phenomenon—a sudden exodus that was soon total and resulted in new concentrations in the Heights areas. Beachwood, for example, several miles to the east, had approximately the same percentage of Jewish students in its high school in the mid-seventies as Glenville had thirty years earlier. Every city witnessed the establishment of new Jewish neighborhoods as a result of movement outward, but in few cases was the new pattern like Cleveland's, with virtually the entire Jewish population extended in a continuous and unbroken line of new settlement forming a kind of crescent from Shaker Heights on the south to Pepper Pike on the east.

The experience in the Kinsman area, Cleveland's other heavily Jewish neighborhood, was both similar and different. There was a comparable sense of neighborhood loyalty;[6] a central institution, the Council Educational Alliance on East 135th Street, to anchor Jewish life; and a sprinkling of small *shuls*, meat markets, and eating places that were also social centers. The barber shops on Kinsman remain in the folk memory as centers of vivid Saturday debates that were characterized by a strongly political and radical accent as well as by their concern with things Jewish. But John Adams High School, the neighborhood school, was never even as much as one quarter Jewish, and the area of the neighborhood was larger, with far more representation from other ethnic groups. Whereas the Glenville area was for many years represented in City Council by three Jewish councilmen (from the 24th, 25th, and 27th wards),[7] the Kinsman area rarely had any Jewish representation in Council throughout the entire period.

It was generally believed—rightly or not
—that the Kinsman neighborhood was
more proletarian, the 105th Street district
more middle class, and the Heights area
for those who had made it. Dating patterns
took note of these distinctions and the
labels "a Kinsman boy," "a Glenville fellow,"
or "He's from the Heights" all carried subtle
nuances of social distinctiveness that replaced earlier designations like *Litvak* or
Galitzianer. Nevertheless, what united
the Jewish community was far more basic
than what divided it, and Cleveland
entered the postwar period with a sense of
a shared common experience and rootedness
not easily achieved in the earlier years when
new waves of immigrants had constantly to
be absorbed. The quarter-century of stability
in the East 105th Street and Kinsman areas
was invaluable in forging a united community.

Economic Explosion

One of the most decisive developments
in the postwar period, affecting every other
phase of communal growth, was the astonishing economic growth of the community.
In the period before 1945 affluence was largely
confined to a small group, long established
and sometimes still referred to as the
Deutsche Yehudim even though some
of them were not actually of German origin.
The establishment of their enterprises in
retailing, in the garment industry, in manufacturing, and in the service industries has
been chronicled elsewhere.

Now a new chapter opened. There was an
explosion of Jewish business activity, most
of it by relative newcomers, many of them
sons of East European parents. Listings on
the stock exchanges provide an insight into
how conditions changed. In 1945 there was
only one listing on the New York or American
Stock Exchange of a Cleveland company

primarily owned by Jews. In 1975 there were
seven such Cleveland companies listed on
the New York exchange and nine on the
American exchange, representing a substantial proportion of new Cleveland concerns
so listed during that period. In addition, many
Jewish-owned businesses went public so
that there were eleven more listed over
the counter.

Growth into larger units was typical; for
example, an informal scrap business might
evolve into a full-fledged smelting business,
and then, after stock had been issued
and the business had grown substantially,
be sold to a still larger concern, usually not
based in Cleveland. Even on more modest
economic levels the same process was taking
place. The small "Mom and Pop" stores disappeared, but the supermarkets that replaced
these little grocery stores and fruit and
vegetable stands were, to a substantial degree, headed by Jewish entrepreneurs—
and the construction and development
companies that so largely determined how the
country changed and grew during the period
were in significant part Jewish-owned as
well.

A curious illustration of this process could
be seen, of all places, in what happened
to the kosher meat markets. In 1947 there
were sixty-three, but by 1975 the number had
declined to twelve. Yet the amount of kosher
meat being sold in them had not diminished!
Obviously, those shops that had survived
had become far larger and did a much greater
volume of business. The dingy, narrow, one-
man shop was gone, and in its place was
a brightly lighted kosher market, skillfully
displaying and packaging its wares,
closed on Saturday nights and Sunday
mornings, formerly the best possible times
for relaxed neighborhood *shmoos* and gossip,
now transferred to the beauty salons.

1.   Frank's Hebrew Book Store, Cleveland Heights. 1975 (Richard E. Karberg)

2.   Cleveland Heights Branch, Jewish Community Center. ca. 1950 (Jewish Community Center)

3.   Bureau of Jewish Education, Cleveland Heights; architects Sigmund Braverman and Moses Halperin; dedicated 1952. 1975 (Richard E. Karberg)

4.   Council Gardens, Cleveland Heights. 1975 (Richard E. Karberg)

Crumbling Barriers

The effect on both the Jewish and the general community of this entrance into the mainstream of Cleveland's economic life was dramatic. Barriers that had seemed impenetrable crumbled. Nowhere was the change more dramatic than in the universities; Western Reserve University (as it was then known) constituted the best example. Although there had been a few Jewish faculty members over the years, by the outbreak of the war there were almost none, despite the fact that there was always a considerable Jewish student body. By the sixties, however, there were Jewish faculty members in substantial numbers at every level in every department.

On the lay side the change was equally impressive. The chairmen of the boards of both Cleveland State University (Joseph Cole) and Cuyahoga Community College (Robert Lewis) were Jewish; so, at one time or another, were the chairman of the Board of Trustees (William C. Treuhaft), the Provost (Herman L. Stein), and the chairman of the Board of Overseers (Henry L. Zucker) of Case Western Reserve University; so was the chairman of the Board of John Carroll University (Frank E. Joseph), a Catholic-sponsored college.

Cleveland had its first Jewish school superintendent, Dr. William B. Levenson (ironically, after all the Jewish students had left for the suburban schools); Jewish doctors were in top positions throughout the city. Those prestigious law firms that were formerly closed to Jewish attorneys without exception began to seek out young Jewish talent.

Almost every business could bear witness to the entry of Jews into fields formerly closed through some form of "gentlemen's agreement" or simply through Jewish acceptance of exclusion as inevitable because it was a tradition so long unchallenged.

In lines of business where they had always been active, Jews now frequently became dominant. Construction and development provide an outstanding example. By 1975 Cuyahoga County was almost completely built up, and the maze of shopping centers and supermarkets and malls and entire new neighborhoods that was so central a feature of Cleveland's growth in the three decades, as it was throughout the country, was in significant degree a Jewish enterprise. Forest City Enterprises, established and controlled by the Ratner family, was clearly the most important developer in the region. Southgate, at the time of its founding the largest shopping center in Northeast Ohio, was built by A. Siegler and Sons. The food and drug and the garment industries were only slightly less spectacular in providing examples of Jewish business initiative.

Only heavy industry—the giants in steel and chemicals and shipping and machine tools—remained largely dominated by traditional elements of the community. By mid-century, banking also witnessed change, though here it was characterized by tokenism. I. F. Freiberger ("Fry") had for decades been an outstanding figure in the world of finance as the chairman of Cleveland Trust Company, the largest bank in Ohio, but his status was unique in a field where few Jews held top posts. Most banks added a Jewish director or two, or a top position employee, and a number of smaller banks were organized by Jews, but the power of the largest banks remained essentially in traditional hands. So did the direction of the major utilities, although here, too, Jews were occasionally added to the boards of directors.

Labor and politics followed a somewhat different course, in both cases as a result of demographic changes. For all practical purposes, the immigrant Jewish constituency in

12 the labor unions (the garment industry, cigar-making, etc.) disappeared. So did the Jewish Painters Union and the Jewish Carpenters Union as the trades lost their hold on a new generation that almost always went to college and opted for the professions, business, or the service industries. A few Jews remained in top positions, but the day of grass roots Jewish participation in union affairs was over.

The picture in politics was more complex. In the late forties there were four Jews (Victor Cohen, Herman Finkle, Harry Jaffe, and Harry Marshall) among the thirty-two members of the Cleveland City Council, the highest number ever. They had held their posts for so many years that they wielded considerable influence on city government. By 1960 there were no Jews on City Council, although three of the four former Jewish members were appointed judges and were subsequently reelected.

Other elective posts followed a curious pattern. Jews were elected to judicial posts in substantial numbers. In 1974 a total of six served on the Common Pleas bench or the Court of Appeals.[8] Although most of them first came on the bench by appointment to fill out unexpired terms, all were subsequently elected. On the other hand, with two exceptions—Alfred A. Benesch, as a long-term member of the Cleveland Board of Education, and Samuel Gerber, as County Coroner—no Jew was elected to a non-judicial office of the county or the city of Cleveland except (as in the case of the councilmen) as the representative of a district. Never was a Jew elected to the office of mayor, county commissioner, or county auditor, or to any other office that required support from the entire community. Nor, for that matter, with a single exception (Gilbert Bettman of Cincinnati, who was elected Attorney General), had any Jew won an office in a statewide election, a situation that is possibly unique among the industrial states of the Union, where Jews reside in sub-

stantial numbers. The situation changed dramatically in 1976 with the election of Howard M. Metzenbaum to the United States Senate. (A number of Jews have been elected to the state legislature, but, again, they have required the support only of their particular districts.) The record contrasts with that of other ethnic groups, including those less numerous. Irish, Italians, Slovenians, blacks, Rumanians can count mayors or county commissioners or similar office-holders among their numbers.

Likewise, experience in the suburbs for the most part reflects little progress toward achieving elective office, indicating either indifference to such participation or a lack of group cohesion or skill. Cleveland Heights and Shaker Heights, the suburbs with the highest number of Jews, have had between them only one Jewish chief officer, Fred Stashower, who served as mayor of Cleveland Heights. There has never been a Jewish majority nor, usually, anything close to it on their city councils or school boards. Until almost 1970 Jewish councilmen in Cleveland Heights began their service through appointment by the traditional group in power, which from time to time selected a Jewish representative. Only in suburbs where the Jewish population became overwhelming, as in University Heights (two-thirds Jewish) or Beachwood (almost ninety percent Jewish), did the various elective offices reflect the constituency. It is not likely that other ethnic groups would be so reluctant to use their political clout.

Nevertheless, it would be inaccurate to assume the absence of Jewish political influence. Many Jewish businesses remained within Cleveland's corporate limits; almost the entire Jewish legal profession, so crucial to political development, had offices in the downtown area; the Jewish Community Federation, when in 1965 it decided it needed its own facility, elected to build on Euclid Avenue and East 18th Street rather than moving to the suburbs, in part to demonstrate its intention to continue to work closely with other community forces in revitalizing the city. The result was that Jewish participation in the political life of the central city continued, although not through direct representation. In almost every contest for office the support of influential Jews was sought by nominees; frequently, Jews served in such top posts as campaign managers, executive assistants, members of the mayor's cabinet, or chairmen of special lay committees.[9] Saul Stillman served for years as one of the four members of the Board of Elections and as co-chairman of the Republican party of the county, replacing in both posts his mentor, Dan Wasserman, who had been appointed to the Court of Appeals. Democrat Howard M. Metzenbaum, elected to the Ohio House of Representatives as the youngest member ever to serve in the state legislature, and subsequently to two terms in the state Senate, became the first Jew to serve in the United States Senate from Ohio. He served by governor's appointment after besting John Glenn in the 1970 primary and losing in the general election to Robert A. Taft, Jr., whom he then defeated in 1976.

Rigid patterns of exclusion were broken in other areas of community life, and again an economic factor was the underlying solvent. Cleveland's symbol of social exclusion was the Union Club, whose forbidding structure and moat-like depressions along Euclid Avenue seemed to proclaim a desire to preserve the way of life of the founders of the Western Reserve. Jewish guests could be invited to the Club, but they could not eat in the main dining room, a gratuitous insult that rankled with Jews and embarrassed Christians and led to recurrent problems when community events or private business meetings were un-thinkingly scheduled to take place there. Most Jews refused such invitations. In the early seventies the policy of exclusion was broken with the invitation to five Jews to membership, followed quickly by further invitations to others. Shortly after, a dinner was given in the main dining room by a major bank in honor of David N. Myers, who was one of its directors and an outstanding Jewish leader. Rabbi Daniel J. Silver, before delivering the traditional blessing, remarked on the sharp break with the Club's past symbolized both by the occasion and by the Hebraic blessing.

The change in policy at the Union Club was a paradigm of what took place in many other areas of Cleveland's cultural, business, civic, and social life. The University Club, the yacht clubs, and similar prestigious social clubs yielded to the changing times, and, at least formally, dropped their barriers against Jews.

Two of Cleveland's most distinguished cultural enterprises, founded by top society and for years the province of the elite, acquired influential Jewish members: the Musical Arts Association, sponsor of the famed Cleveland Orchestra, elected Frank E. Joseph as its president and later as chairman of its Board of Trustees; and the Cleveland Museum of Art increasingly added key Jewish members both to its Board of Directors and to its staff. A third prestigious cultural organization, the Cleveland Play House, was open from its founding and has elected three Jewish presidents—Louis Rorimer, Jay Iglauer, and Harold Fallon. The Cleveland Institute of Music throughout its history has had substantial Jewish participation, and the same is true of the Karamu Theater. Serving particularly the black community, Karamu at one point in the seventies had a Jewish president (Sidney Josephs) and a Jewish director (Reuben Silver), both also active in the

Taylor Road Synagogue, Cleveland Heights; architect Milo Holdstein; dedicated 1951. (Jewish Community Federation)

Jewish community. It was, however, a situation not likely to recur, as black insistence on reserving such posts for its own members became fixed policy.

In the field of creative writing there had of course never been barriers, and the list of Cleveland Jews whose writings became nationally significant is impressive. It includes the novelists Herbert Gold and Julius Horwitz; the dramatist Jerome Lawrence (*Inherit the Wind*); Jo Sinclair (Ruth Seid), winner of the Harper Prize for *Wasteland*, the story of an immigrant Jewish family; Gerold Frank, co-author of numerous Hollywood autobiographies and author of *The Pledge*, a novel about the Stern Gang; David Miller, whose *The Chain and the Link* recaptured life in the *shtetl*; Richard Howard, Pulitzer prize poet; Joseph S. Newman, master of light verse; and many others. Almost all made the Cleveland Jewish scene the background for important parts of their work. David B. Guralnik, for many years editor of the *New World Dictionary of the American Language*, became an internationally recognized authority on lexicography. In journalism, Jews were well represented on both the city's newspapers, most notably by David Dietz, Pulitzer prize winner in journalism and science editor of the Scripps-Howard newspapers.

At the other end of the cultural spectrum, the city's two most prestigious sports teams were headed by Jews. Arthur Modell became the principal owner of the Cleveland Browns (football), and Alva T. Bonda headed the Cleveland Indians (baseball) with a group of partners, many of whom were also Jewish. To the man on the street, this was a significant indication that Jews had arrived.

To trace the breakthroughs in other areas of the city's life would be to list almost every civic enterprise. The City Club, the Citizen's League, the Growth Association (successor to the Chamber of Commerce), the bar associa-

tions, the medical societies, the United Way, the Welfare Federation (later the Federation for Community Planning), and innumerable other leading organizations had substantial Jewish representation, including high officers. Morton L. Mandel, on completing his term as president of the Jewish Community Federation, was elected to the same post by the United Way. Even the more closed groups, such as the Fifty Club, an organization of the leading and most influential businessmen, had Jews among their members.

Nor was the involvement in the general community paid for by desertion of the Jewish community. The story of two "Mikes" graphically illustrates the simultaneous assumption of leadership in both communities. Myron "Mike" Guren served as president of both the Jewish Community Center and the U.S.O.; M. E. "Mike" Glass as president of both the Jewish Community Federation and the League for Human Rights. Also typical of the spread of leadership was the fact that both men, among many other offices, served as president of their synagogue.

What explains so sweeping a penetration, in so short a time, after a century of little progress? No doubt most basic was the change in American outlook—toward a more open society, accessible to all sections of the community. But the dramatic upward economic movement of Jews, which exceeded the national pace, is also explained by the fact that in this period American Jewry became almost totally native born, well educated, and thoroughly at home in American life. The Jewish community moved to the top of all ethnic or native groups in average income, and Cleveland participated fully in this leap forward.[10]

It would be easy but misleading to overstate the Jewish influence. Undertakings of crucial importance in the city's life remained in the hands of the group descended

16 from the original settlers, largely Protestant and North European, but now the Jewish input and the Jewish potential and the Jewish readiness to back new ideas were so valuable that they could not easily be overlooked. As associations grew and joint efforts paid off, Jews achieved a degree of participation that contrasted sharply with their former isolation. But participation in no way implies domination. Demography alone would have made that impossible. Jews constituted only four percent of the area's population in the mid-seventies, down from an earlier proportion that approached ten percent in the twenties.

In any case, economic forces were not alone responsible for normalizing the Jewish position in the community. A second major factor was the sweeping change in American life and outlook brought about by the civil rights movement. The Cleveland Jewish community, like others throughout the country, played a leading role in the successive campaigns to break barriers of discrimination. In 1945 the Jewish Community Council and the local chapter of the National Association for the Advancement of Colored People formed an intimate partnership resulting in two decades of joint leadership for the civil rights movement that ended abruptly with the advent of more turbulent times in the mid-sixties. Their first achievement was the establishment, in 1945, of a City of Cleveland Community Relations Board, the third in the country and the first to be established as an official arm of city government. Max Simon, later to be president of both the Jewish Community Council and the Jewish Community Federation, and Abraham Rubin served on the founding board. Among their successors were Ben D. Zevin, Irving Kane, and Jordan C. Band, all highly active in the Jewish community, as well as Morris Rieger and Max Amdur.

Most notably Ezra Z. Shapiro became head of the Board in 1963 (technically, vice-chairman, since the Mayor by law was titular chairman) and served until he moved to Israel in 1971. In 1951, after a two-year experiment with a "voluntary plan," Cleveland City Council established one of the first municipal Fair Employment Practices Commissions in the country outside of the eastern seaboard. It took this step at a dramatic session, during which NAACP and Jewish leadership reported that in urging the legislation, they had been joined by leaders of the Chamber of Commerce, formerly strongly opposed to such action. It marked the first occasion anywhere that a business organization had joined in requesting the passage of such legislation.

The legislative campaigns for civil rights then shifted to the state arena, where the same Cleveland "team" provided leadership in a series of efforts that failed despite intensive and often innovative campaigning, and often by frustratingly close votes in four successive biennial sessions of the legislature, starting in 1949. Then, suddenly, conditions changed. In 1959 the legislature enacted a statute establishing a Civil Rights Commission, with power to enforce a Fair Employment Practices Act; in 1961 a Fair Public Accommodations Act was passed; in 1963, a Fair Housing statute. After four defeats, three successive victories!

The campaigns were sparked jointly by the NAACP and the Jewish Community Council and later by the Federation; support came from the growing backing of religious, civic, labor, and, finally, many business organizations.

With the passage of these three statutes, the basic legislative tools had been provided. Moreover, the thrust for civil rights was enormously strengthened by subsequent executive actions and federal legislation. Irving Kane, then president of the National Community Relations Advisory Council, was a key leader in the campaign for federal legislation. In the case of later affirmative action programs, more than equal treatment, and greater minority opportunity became established as government policy. The effects this policy would later have upon both the Jewish and the general community were totally unforeseen and unpredictable.

Action now shifted from legislation to litigation. Discrimination in housing was the area in which Jews had encountered the greatest difficulties. Whole sections of the suburbs—notably in the "Club District" bordering Warrensville Road, and in Pepper Pike—remained closed to Jews, largely as the result of the so-called Van Sweringen restrictions. The name derived from two bachelor brothers, O.P. and M.J. Van Sweringen, who not only dominated Cleveland's economic life in the twenties but became major figures on the national scene until their elaborate schemes collapsed in bankruptcy during the Depression. What remained as a permanent and visible memorial to them (in addition to the Terminal Tower, still Cleveland's show building and a kind of logo for the city) was the conversion of Shaker Heights from a sleepy village into a showplace city, a symbol of affluence.

To guarantee continuing status and prestige for their elegant suburb, the land company they established included restrictions on the titles of many homes or vacant lots under their control. The restrictions, which continued to control a major part of Shaker Heights and Pepper Pike even after the bankruptcy, required the consent of immediate neighbors on both sides of the street before owners could dispose of their property. In practice, they proved a good device for keeping out the "unwanted," which in most cases meant Jews and blacks.

The exclusion took a somewhat exotic form in Pepper Pike, one of the most prestigious

far eastern suburbs. There the city fathers established as informal public policy that no more than one in four homes could be sold to Jews. They claimed such a twenty-five percent sharing of home ownership was in reality a mark of liberalism, since Jews constituted a far smaller percentage of the population. But such "liberalism" grated on many Jewish nerves sensitized over the centuries against quota arrangements.

By the late fifties artificial restraints on housing were under attack, as lawmakers, courts, and executive bodies followed and broadened the action taken by the Supreme Court in its 1954 school desegregation decision. In Cleveland the most dramatic action was a successful law suit by the city's oldest congregation, the Euclid Avenue Temple (later the Fairmount Temple). Legally, the issue was whether a religious organization had the right to build in an area zoned for private housing only. But what was also involved—and primarily involved—was reluctance at having the Jewish penetration into the eastern suburbs facilitated by the building of a major new synagogue that would be certain to attract substantial Jewish settlement.

The case was argued up to the Ohio Supreme Court by Morris Berick, generally recognized as among the outstanding legal scholars in the region. The result was a verdict for the synagogue and the subsequent erection of a magnificent structure on Fairmount Boulevard, east of Green Road (at that time representing the furthest penetration east of any Jewish communal building). The new Fairmount Temple soon became a favored meeting place for Jewish communal events as well as a center for congregational activities.

The new temple's architect was Percival Goodman. A decade earlier, Eric Mendelsohn had designed the nationally acclaimed Park Synagogue (formerly the Jewish Center) on that congregation's beautifully wooded grounds in Cleveland Heights, while a decade later, the new Jewish Community Federation building downtown and the B'rith Emeth structure in Pepper Pike, even further east than Fairmount Temple, would be designed by Edward Durell Stone. Cleveland Jewry thus contributed edifices planned by three of the nation's outstanding architects, another symbol of the community's maturation.

A more direct blow to the Van Sweringen restrictions was the Supreme Court's decision that such restraints on the individual owner's right to sell his property were legally unenforceable. The result was dramatic and ironic. Beachwood, the site of the new Fairmount Temple, became the most concentrated Jewish settlement of all the suburbs. The so-called "Club District" of Shaker Heights, until then for all practical purposes without Jews, became heavily populated by Jews. By the seventies Jews were free to live whereever their pocketbooks permitted. It was a dramatic change even from 1962, when Jordan C. Band, then Chairman of the Community Relations Committee, had testified before the Ohio Civil Rights Commission:

Although discrimination against Jews in the field of housing is certainly not so severe as that directed against Negroes, it is in our judgment a fair generalization to state that there is significant and, in some areas, substantial discrimination in housing against persons of the Jewish faith.

This discrimination falls essentially into four categories: . . . their occupancy of a given residence requires approval by a street or neighborhood committee . . . as in the Forest Hills area of Cleveland Heights and East Cleveland; . . . the unusual type of discrimination in Pepper Pike; . . . the so-called "colony" developments, such as Landerwood, Lyndhurst Park Estates, and others requiring a purchaser to be approved by the colony organizations; . . . and most common and pervasive, the "gentlemen's agreement" of small groups of homeowners.

Housing patterns in suburban areas reveal the in-

creasing tendency of our religious groups to "cluster;" . . . sections of the Heights area are overwhelmingly Jewish; Parma is largely Catholic, Gates Mills is almost entirely Protestant. . . . It is unmistakable that real estate professionals have added to this tendency to cluster by suggesting that there are "Jewish neighborhoods," "Catholic neighborhoods," and "Protestant neighborhoods" and they show homes or refrain from showing homes depending upon religious affiliation. . . . Where to live should be a matter of individual choice and real estate salesmen ought not to suggest the desirability of moving into a religiously homogeneous neighborhood.[11]

It was not until the end of 1975, after a number of law suits and innumerable conferences, that the real estate organizations themselves decided to adopt a policy of "opening up" all areas of the county, including the West Side.

Stabilization

The extraordinary mobility of both the Jewish and the general communities led to a number of topsy-turvy situations. East Cleveland, which for decades had the reputation of being one of the suburbs most hostile to blacks, became almost totally black; neighboring Cleveland Heights, founded by an elitist group that for many years carefully kept control in its own hands, became the suburb most experimental and liberal in publicly seeking integration.

The Jewish community, too, found itself faced by unprecedented new conditions. It had always taken the inevitability of rapid neighborhood change for granted and had directed its communal energies toward making the shifts as smooth as possible as it broke through rings of exclusion that increased in intensity the further east Jews moved. In the late forties, for example, the leadership of the Jewish Community Council met with all the Orthodox congrega-

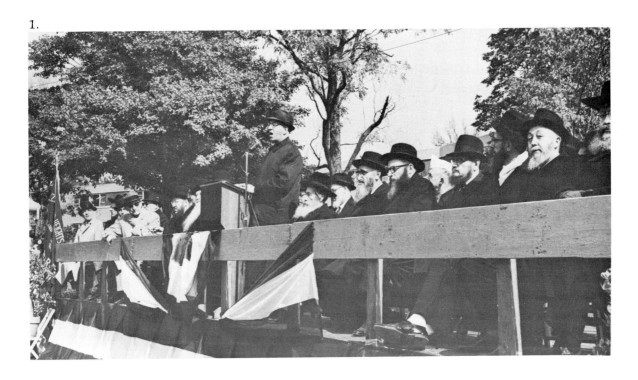

1. In 1956 Telshe Yeshiva acquired the James B. Kirby estate in Wickliffe, Ohio, where it continues to flourish as an influential center of Orthodox religious learning. Shown are groundbreaking ceremonies for new Telshe buildings at the Wickliffe campus; leaders of the Yeshiva listen to remarks by Rabbi Louis Engelberg. October 10, 1964. (Berni Rich)

2. Interior of the new *Beth Hamidrash* (House of Study). 1966 (Berni Rich)

tions still largely clustered along East 105th Street and adjoining streets in an attempt to help them plan their moves into the Heights area. It was taken for granted that the move was both inevitable and desirable, and the concentration was on effecting mergers wherever possible so that the new buildings to be constructed would be established with a larger membership base in the new area, eliminating the fragmentation and occasional store-front, temporary facilities of the previous era. The rapid increase in costs as congregational responsibilities grew made such combinations fiscally inevitable, and the decline of separate ethnic traditions ("the Litvisher *shul*", "the Hungarian *shul*," etc.) made such distinctions merely humorous— no longer a valid ground for separation. The new Taylor Road Synagogue, the Heights Jewish Center, and, somewhat later, the Warrensville Road Synagogue all represented absorption or combinations of smaller units into larger, more viable ones.

By 1970, however, the prospect of still another major move was viewed quite differently. With barriers thoroughly broken, concern was more directed toward stabilizing neighborhoods and attempting to forestall the difficulties caused by the continuous movement outward. Jewish institutions had been established in Cleveland Heights in an even more concentrated fashion than in the old days on East 105th Street and on a far more sophisticated and expensive level. Taylor Road had become the new main Jewish thoroughfare, particularly central to the Orthodox community. The Hebrew Academy (the Orthodox all-day school) and Taylor Road Synagogue became the new anchor points for an impressive number of *shuls* and bakeries and delicatessens serving Orthodox needs. The area became the only location in Cleveland where Saturday meant closed business establishments, lessened traffic, and a general

atmosphere of religious observance reflecting the spirit of the Sabbath. Liberal Orthodoxy was represented through the vigorous Young Israel movement, which also added immeasurably to the Jewish life clustered around Taylor Road.

Nor was the new concentration characteristic only of the Orthodox community. Also on or adjoining Taylor Road were the buildings of the Jewish Family Service Association and the Bureau of Jewish Education, toward the south; and, to the north, the Jewish Community Center and the Council Gardens, founded by the Council of Jewish Women to house independent elderly persons. Slightly to the west were the two major Conservative congregations, Park Synagogue and the Temple on the Heights, as well as the Montefiore Home for the Aged. Never in the history of the community had there been such a concentration of major Jewish institutions.

Small wonder that the prospect of further movement had its threatening aspects. It was one thing to replace structures on East 105th Street or Kinsman—rather simple facilities, with the exception of the massive Jewish Center—which were erected by a generation committed to quick movement and accustomed to putting up buildings for fast use and fast disposal. It was quite another matter to contemplate replacing highly expensive edifices, many of them elaborately planned, elegantly executed, and designed for long-term utilization. Moreover, the general neighborhood remained a desirable location, with good facilities and services and schools. Finally, the former widely held assumptions of the inevitability and desirability of growth and change and newness were being increasingly challenged. The challenge took on highly tangible dimensions when it was estimated that relocating the Jewish institutions would require an expenditure of a hundred million dollars, to say nothing of the fiscal and human

Dr. Harry Goldbatt, noted kidney researcher, and Dr. Erwin Haas, directors of the Louis D. Beaumont Memorial Research Laboratories. ca. 1973 (Mt. Sinai Hospital)

price exacted if Jewish homeowners and businesses, many of them in relatively modest circumstances, were forced to seek new housing in more expensive neighborhoods.

Faced by these considerations, the Jewish Community Federation undertook an innovative program that came to be known as the Cleveland Heights Project. It began in 1969 at a meeting called by the president of the Federation at which representatives of almost all Jewish institutions in the area declared their intention to remain in the neighborhood. (The Temple on the Heights was a major exception; the first Jewish religious institution to move "up the hill"—in 1922—it had already announced plans to move to a new location further east.)

The well-publicized joint declaration to stay put, an unprecedented event in communal history, was itself an important contribution to neighborhood stability. But more concrete measures were undertaken: a mortgage assistance program to help prospective homeowners to purchase homes in the area, a public relations program, creation of street clubs, active cooperation with and stimulation of city government to provide key services and meet new needs. Perhaps most important was constant contact with both public and other private institutions in the area, culminating in the creation of a city-wide Cleveland Heights Congress of many religious, racial, and civic groups united to preserve the suburb's standards while simultaneously insuring that it was open to all. Stabilization *and* integration were the objectives. A full-time staff was employed by the Federation to implement the elaborate program.

The commitment to neighborhood stability was best demonstrated by a controversial Federation decision in 1973 requiring the Bureau of Jewish Education to remain in its building on Taylor Road rather than moving, as previously planned, with the College of

Jewish Studies when that sister institution in 1975 completed its new facility in an outlying location on Shaker Boulevard. The step, in unusual contravention of the traditional policy favoring the right of an agency to select its own location, demonstrated that the organized community was prepared to take hard decisions to help prevent or at least slow down the shifts in population that had characterized earlier communal history. How lasting such steps would be over the course of the years was still unclear, since Cleveland Heights in the decade 1965–1975 changed considerably, with substantial growth in black population and a corresponding decline in Jewish population. Certainly panic selling had been avoided, and change was taking place at a viable pace, in contrast to the situation in neighboring East Cleveland, but the reasons, including a recession that slowed down home purchases, were complex. Nevertheless, enough had been accomplished to encourage many homeowners and institutions to remain rooted if they wished to do so. The Cleveland Heights Project became a model to communities throughout the country eager to retain Jewish neighborhoods in inner-ring suburbs, while avoiding any suggestion of organizing to keep out other groups, particularly blacks, also seeking to enter the neighborhood.

Community Relationships

Relations with the black community form one of the most checkered and volatile components of Jewish history of the period. Until the Second World War the two communities, then roughly equal in size, had little formal relationship. There were the traditional personal relationships—Jewish landlord and black (or, in those days, Negro) tenant; Jewish merchant and black customer; Jewish housewife and black housekeeper. (A bit later, many thrift shops were established by Jewish women's organizations in predominantly black areas.) No doubt there existed the resentments and irritations and prejudices inevitable in such unequal relationships, but there is no reason to doubt that the situation in Cleveland reflected the findings of national polls in the fifties indicating that black attitudes were, despite reservations, more favorable to Jews than to other whites. Certainly the breakouts from the black ghetto were largely into Jewish neighborhoods. They were frequently accompanied by statements from the newcomers that only among Jewish neighbors could they feel relatively safe from overt community hostility. With good reason. In contrast to developments in the so-called ethnic neighborhoods, there is no record of any Jewish organized movement to keep out "the unwanted," nor of any Jew involved in racial violence. Indeed, the organized movements for integration, notably in the Ludlow and Lomond districts in Shaker Heights, were in or adjacent to Jewish neighborhoods, with Jewish neighbors prominent in their leadership.

From a population of about 100,000 in 1940, the number of blacks in Cleveland grew dramatically until it reached well over 350,000 by 1975; blacks became a majority of the school population of Cleveland, and, as we have seen, moved in significant numbers into almost every suburb where Jews lived. Under the impact of national and international as well as local events, the black community began to expand its existing institutions, to develop new ones, and in general to conduct itself increasingly *as* a community.

The impact on the Jewish community was significant. The first phase, from 1945 to about 1960, was one of partnership and generally good inter-community feeling. The joint campaign for civil rights led an NAACP executive to remark, "I thought of the Jewish Community Council as my downtown office and my own NAACP as my uptown office." Rabbi Arthur Lelyveld of Fairmount Temple, one of many Jews who actively joined in the civil rights marches in the South, suffered a severe physical attack there and returned to Cleveland a hero of the black community and a leading symbol of dedicated liberalism. Other rabbis and community leaders, lay and professional, participated vigorously in programs aimed at black rights and progress; campaigns for black organizations were generously aided by Jews. Councilman (later Judge) George White led a black delegation to the Jewish Community Federation to learn how to forge a community organization, and subsequently created a "Negro Community Federation" which completely mirrored the Jewish model, despite advice that the needs, experience, and operations of the two communities were so dissimilar that a simple imitation of one by the other was doomed to failure, as indeed proved to be the case.

Relations changed in the second half of the sixties. Romantic expectations, aroused by the 1954 Supreme Court desegregation decision and kept alive for a decade by the excitement of successful legislative campaigns and the drama of confrontations in the South, soured as problems of achieving integration in the North proved complicated and at times intractable. The schools in Cleveland became more, not less, segregated as whites took off for the suburbs. In the mid-sixties the increasingly frustrated and militant blacks formed the United Freedom Movement. Its chief goal was to pressure the Cleveland Board of Education to take a variety of steps to fight segregation, although its stated objective was simply to provide an ongoing mechanism to fight for equal rights for all. Originally, it was composed of representatives of all three religious groups—Jewish, Catholic, and Protestant—

24 as well as several civic organizations and a whole gamut of black organizations. But, as demands for change grew more insistent and the resistance to change stronger, there were violent confrontations between the UFM and supporters of the conservative school board. Finally the new movement sponsored a boycott of the schools; "Freedom Schools" were created to replace them. The climax came suddenly in the shocking death of a young and attractive Protestant clergyman inadvertently run over by a tractor during a protest against construction of a new school, allegedly to be at a location that would promote continued segregation. Violence escalated, erupting in 1969 in shoot-outs in Glenville, the former Jewish district, that terrorized the entire city and ended only when the National Guard was called in.

The era of good feeling ended as militants took over with demands that gradually alienated most white participants. The policy of the Jewish Community Federation was defined at a meeting of its Board of Trustees: "Our role . . . has been to function with a combination of commitment and caution." But the times and the chief actors in this drama were impatient with any such policy of "deliberate speed."[12]

There was still some residue of good feeling: *The Call and Post*, the black newspaper, remained consistently friendly to Israel; the older generation of black political leaders retained close ties to opposite numbers in the Jewish community; and improvements in welfare and humanitarian standards, of crucial importance to blacks, were vigorously supported by all three major religious groups. Nevertheless, the honeymoon had given way to bleak reality. The former assumption that each generation would be more understanding and sympathetic about racial differences than its predecessors proved erroneous. As young blacks proclaimed their rejection of integration as a desirable objective, school-

boy fights along racial lines accelerated, Third World philosophy permeated the black community more deeply, and Jewish liberalism grew less universal. The partnership of black and Jewish interests had served both communities well in eliminating many artificial barriers to individual achievement and in developing a more sympathetic understanding of the vital role of ethnicity. How that partnership could be reshaped to meet the problems of the last quarter of the century was still unresolved in 1975.

Religious Relationships

Relations with other religious communities during the period followed a sharply different course, becoming markedly closer over the years, particularly with the Catholic community. In 1945 the immigrant heritage of uneasiness and distrust concerning institutional religion was still strong. Perhaps more than any other American city, Cleveland was made up of ethnic, mostly Catholic, groups. More foreign language papers were printed in Cleveland than in any other American city except New York, and attitudes of separation characteristic of East European countries set the pattern for both Jews and Christians. The National Conference of Christians and Jews had been organized in Cleveland in the late twenties, and its annual Brotherhood Week celebrations were ceremoniously observed. Politics and business provided points of contact, as did the inevitable mingling in the neighborhoods. Nevertheless, "the Church" was hardly regarded as friendly, and contacts were severely limited by the "five o'clock shadow." The almost total absence of Jews from the West Side, where the Church's influence was strongest, was significant.

Relations with the Protestant community were much closer. Exchanges of pulpits between rabbis and ministers were common; the annual Institute on Judasim sponsored

1.

2.

3.

4.

1. Cedar-Center, University Heights. 1977 (Richard E. Karberg)

2. Entrance to Menorah Park; window by Ben Shahn. (David Hirsch, New York)

3. Exterior of Menorah Park, Jewish Home for the Aged, Beachwood; dedicated 1968. (David Hirsch, New York)

4. Editorial cartoon. 1948 (Cleveland *Plain Dealer*)

The Bellefaire campus, University Heights. 1959 (Lynn Rebman)

by the Euclid Avenue Temple (Fairmount Temple) was so well attended by the Ministerial Alliance that each year its members held their regular monthly meeting there on that date; the Church Federation, the coordinating Protestant organization, worked far more closely with the organized Jewish community than did the Catholic Diocese. Correctly or not, the Protestant tradition generally associated with the Anglo-Saxon countries was seen as less threatening and more open than the Catholic tradition of eastern Europe.

As late as 1961, the religious relationships were summarized in "Cleveland, City Without Jews"[13] as follows:

1. Little overt conflict exists, and there is a pervasive atmosphere of avoiding tension situations. As a result, there is little "dialogue" among religious groups, and the price of relatively little conflict is relatively shallow interreligious contacts. Blandness is the key everywhere.

2. Close interreligious cooperation, where it exists, is rarely on specifically religious projects. It is more likely to occur on civic, philanthropic, and business levels.

3. The Roman Catholic community is the most isolated of the three major faith groups. The Archbishop explains the withdrawal: "Our inferiority complex reveals itself even today in the tendency to isolate ourselves from the community as a whole." There is only now, with the beginning of an interreligious dialogue, faint stirring toward increasing participation. These efforts are sparked by Catholic laymen.

4. Each religious group has issues in which it is primarily interested: The Catholic priority is increased policing of the mass media and gaining support for their schools; the Protestant, changing neighborhoods; the Jewish, church-state relationships. Closest cooperation exists, particularly between liberal Protestants and Jews, in the area of civil rights.

5. Almost all areas of daily living reflect an increasing sifting down into religious compartments. Churches and synagogues have become more central institutions; schools, housing and social satisfactions are likely to follow religious lines. Even employment and (to a lesser degree) business patterns have increasingly an element of religious self-segregation. Weekly ads in the diocesan paper seem to symbolize the strange ways of this apartness: "Low cost of hospitalization," it emphasizes in large headlines, "available only to Ohio Catholics."

6. The white population of all three religious groups is becoming increasingly suburban. Despite the growth of religious institutions and the separateness that has been described, religious issues and values seem to count less than the absorbing interest in material satisfactions that characterize all three groups. The "things" of suburban living outweigh religious values or differentiation.

The following fifteen years brought great changes, particularly in the Catholic community. Reflecting both the new international openness generally associated with the influence of Pope John XXIII and strong pressures at home that saw nuns join picket lines and priests and Catholic laymen become deeply involved in programs of social action, Catholic and Jewish cooperation and contacts greatly increased. Dialogues became commonplace on both ministerial and lay levels; a Conference on Religion and Race brought representatives of all three religious groups into active cooperation on a variety of issues. When Carl Stokes, first black mayor of any major city, felt it necessary in 1969 to conduct a survey of public welfare in Cleveland, he called on the three religious groups to supply both the funds and much of the manpower for the study. (Dr. Herman L. Stein, then provost of Case Western Reserve University and highly active in the Jewish community, served as chairman.) Frank E. Joseph was elected chairman of the Board of Overseers of John Carroll University; Marvin Zelman, formerly lay head of the Jewish Family Service Association, was elected head of the Catholic Family Association; and it became unremarkable for a Jew to be named Man of

28 the Year by Catholic organizations. The *Catholic Universe Bulletin's* articles and editorials on Israel were eloquent in their support of Jewish interests. The diocesan office, once glacially distant, was now cordial and open. In the Heights area, meetings took place alternately at Jewish institutions and in Catholic churches and even monasteries, inasmuch as the interest of both groups in preserving the neighborhood coincided.

Protestant relationships did not have so much isolation to overcome and did not progress so dramatically. Although cooperation and general good feeling persisted, the organized Protestant community became in the decade 1965–1975 increasingly attuned to the more militant mood described earlier in the discussion of the black community. The views of the Catholic and Jewish communities on how to effect social change grew closer and increasingly differed from those of the more activist Protestant community, in contrast to the situation a generation earlier, when Protestant and Jewish interests more frequently coincided.

Summary

The thirty-year period 1945–1975 was one of unparalleled progress for the Cleveland Jewish community in almost every phase of the city's life—economic, social, educational, vocational, and, with some reservations, political. Indeed, the assimilation of the now native-born Jewish population had gone so far that it was regarded as a mixed blessing by those concerned with the rapid increase in intermarriage and what they regarded as decay in Jewish literacy and commitment that would inevitably threaten community life. To determine the validity of such concerns we must turn to an assessment of the internal developments in the Jewish community during the same period.

Internal Developments

Impact of World Events

IN an address delivered at the annual
meeting of the Jewish Community Federation in 1956, Henry L. Zucker, its Executive
Vice President, reviewed the decade of postwar
communal experience then ending and concluded:

During this ten-year period, the work . . . has
been dominated by needs of rescue, relief, rehabilitation and reunion of Jews throughout the world.
In concert with Jews from many communities and
countries, [we] helped finance and administer one
of the greatest mass migrations in world history.
. . .

During this period, American Jewry raised more
than a billion dollars, probably the greatest
philanthropic record in history. Cleveland was a
leader in this tremendous effort.[14]

Even these brave claims seemed by comparison with the far greater accomplishments
of the next two decades to be understatements.
The national Jewish community in 1967 set itself the task of raising half a billion dollars,
not in half a decade but in a single year, and
in the seventies actually produced year after
year sums that ranged from a quarter to a half-
billion dollars. The Cleveland contribution to
that gigantic effort was outstanding. In 1946
its Jewish Welfare Fund raised $2,650,000,
more than doubling the 1945 total; twenty
years later a new record was established of
$6,270,000, with the total amount raised in
the two decades of the fifties and sixties exceeding $100,000,000. In 1974, under the
impact of the Yom Kippur War of October,

1973, the staggering total of more than
$23,000,000 was raised in a single campaign.
This outpouring of material support was only
one part of the communal dedication to meeting overseas needs and, more specifically, to
aiding Israel.

The culmination of tensions in the Middle
East in the Six-Day War of 1967 brought major
public relations repercussions. An Israel Task
Force was created in that year, originally
under the chairmanship of Irving Kane (then
also chairman of the American Israel Public
Affairs Committee) and, from 1971 on, under
Rabbi Daniel J. Silver. It coordinated the
many efforts to interpret Israel's concerns and
problems to the media, business, labor, the
schools, the ethnic and black communities,
academia—in short, to all groups where
public opinion was being shaped.

Many individuals became their own "task
forces" through their particular overseas
interests. Max Ratner became president of the
American Israel Chamber of Commerce and,
together with other members of the Ratner
family that played so leading a role in the
community, demonstrated through the formation of Petrochemicals, Ltd. in the industrial
region near Haifa his favorite thesis: in
the long run investments in Israel are even
more crucial to its economic future than
philanthropy. Nevertheless, the Ratner
family's gifts to many Israeli institutions, but
particularly to Hebrew University and Tel
Aviv University, were monumental in themselves and helped spark many other contributions. Irving Stone founded the settlement Telshe-Stone outside Jerusalem as a

30 demonstration village for Orthodox settlement and learning; Max and Eva Apple created and supported a children's village at Gan Yavne, south of Tel Aviv; the Jack, Joseph and Morton Mandel families established a community center at Kiryat Yam near Haifa; and Kfar Silver was founded in honor of the world renowned Cleveland Zionist leader, Rabbi Abba Hillel Silver. Meanwhile numerous Clevelanders were charmed by the exuberant mayor of Jerusalem, Teddy Kollek, and expressed their admiration in a variety of gifts for projects in that city.

Local campaigns for Israel bonds raised millions of dollars every year and involved almost every congregation and local organization in their effort. During this period the Federation participated in a number of bank loans to international agencies totalling $30,000,000 as Cleveland's share in helping meet the huge costs for absorbing immigrants into the new state. Moreover, it twice made million-dollar gifts from its endowment funds in times of emergency, all this in addition to the yearly Welfare Fund Campaigns. The annual meetings of the Jewish National Fund, for decades under the direction of its president, the persistent and indomitable Julius Amber, brought together packed houses of Cleveland's political, legal, and judicial personalities as well as hundreds of workers who purchased "interests" in Israel ranging from single trees to whole forests. Both the Jewish Community Center and the Federation employed full-time *shlichim* (emissaries from Israel) to direct interpretive programs; the Bureau of Jewish Education sponsored summer study tours for hundreds of young Clevelanders; travel to Israel became so common that El Al Airlines established a regional office in Cleveland.

This ferment of activity had markedly different effects on the men's and women's Zionist organizations. Membership in the men's organizations grew steadily in the period before the formation of the state and peaked at about 10,000 with Israel's declaration of independence in 1948. It then declined sharply and steadily to less than a thousand in 1975. In contrast, Hadassah, Pioneer Women, and Mizrachi Women retained both their membership and their programs.

Ironically, the success of "Zionism," in the broad sense of support for Israel, was probably the chief cause of the weakening of the organized men's Zionist movement. After 1948 almost the entire community joined in contributing to the Welfare Fund and in participating in the many activities briefly noted above. To many supporters of Israel, there seemed less need to join a formal structure when there were so many opportunities to express convictions in highly tangible (if less philosophical and ideological) ways. The slogan, "We Are All Zionists," coined in 1976 in reaction to the United Nations resolution linking Zionism with racism, had been demonstrated in practice through the years.

In contrast, all three women's Zionist organizations continued to hold "donors" (fund-raising events), to initiate specific projects, to accept "quotas," and to conduct cultural programs. Evidently, these highly concrete activities provided more nourishing sustenance than the men's groups were able to derive from their programs.

A dramatic symbol of Israel's impact on the thinking of the community and on its own self-image has been the change in the attitude toward teaching Hebrew in the public schools. Attempts to introduce it as a modern language in the school curriculum were made as early as the thirties, culminating in a revealing debate in 1938 at the Bureau of Jewish Education. A number of speakers had urged that the Cleveland Board of Education be formally petitioned to include Hebrew as a

2.

1. President Philmore Haber at meeting of Executive Committee, Jewish Community Council. 1943 (Jewish Community Federation)

2. Jewish Community Council Arts Festival Drama, "The Treasure." 1947 (Jewish Community Federation)

32 subject in the high schools. A highly respected
lawyer, a pillar of the community noted for his
good works in the general as well as the
Jewish community, advised delay:

> I love to foster the Hebrew language . . .[but]
> the time is inopportune to introduce this matter.
> . . . We should be fighting to assert our rights,
> yet . . . I think if we present this proposal at this
> time, we are going to fan certain unreasoning
> elements—the rising tide of anti-Semitism. . . . . .
> We are going to antagonize a very large group of
> people in this community who should be consulted.
> I have spoken to a number of men and every one
> of them is of the opinion that this should not be
> undertaken at this time.[15]

For a variety of reasons, the matter was not
pressed further at that time, and Hebrew was
never introduced into the school curriculum of
Cleveland proper. By the 1950s, however,
defensive attitudes had passed into history,
and despite considerable initial reluctance by
the Cleveland Heights school system (based
largely on the fact that demand for foreign
languages in general was declining) and a
number of delaying tactics, the course was
introduced there in 1954; subsequently it became part of the Beachwood curriculum as well.
Ulpanim (Hebrew courses emphasizing the
spoken language) became the most popular
offering at the College of Jewish Studies, with
almost 200 students, a typical number, at-
tending classes in 1975; in addition, many
congregations conducted their own Hebrew
language courses.

The ties between Cleveland and world Jewry
involved personalities as well as organizations.
The most glittering example, of course, was
Rabbi Abba Hillel Silver's role in the establishment of the state of Israel. His speech before
the United Nations in 1947 on behalf of the
Jewish Agency, presenting the case for parti-
tion of Palestine into independent states,
remains a classic exposition of Jewish
aspiration. Others followed in his tradition.

Edward Ginsberg became head of the United
Jewish Appeal and later of the American
Jewish Joint Distribution Committee (JDC).
Ezra Z. Shapiro was chosen as president of the
Keren Hayesod, an international fund-raising
organization for Israel. Irving Kane was
elected chairman of the American Israel Public
Affairs Committee and was designated honor-
ary vice chairman of the JDC. Rose Kaufman
became the president of Pioneer Women, and
Isabel Brown was elected president of the
International Council of Jewish Women.

In 1957, at the invitation of the American
Jewish Joint Distribution Committee, Henry
L. Zucker undertook a study of European Jewish communities just becoming reestablished
after the pulverizing effects of the war. His
extended analysis was a key contribution to the
establishment of the Standing Conference on
European Communal Service. In 1975 he conducted a second study, this time of the JDC
itself, leading to a redefinition of almost every
phase of the operation of that venerable worldwide organization for Jewish rescue and rehabilitation. Sidney Z. Vincent, Federation
Executive Director, served as Coordinator of
the 1969 Conference on Human Needs in
Jerusalem, which helped establish the pattern
for reorganization of the Jewish Agency several
years later through its then novel technique
of involving representatives of Jewish communities throughout the world in panels to
assess and deal with major problems con-
fronting the Agency.

By broadening the horizons of the Jewish
community, this massive involvement in matters of worldwide concern also encouraged a
growing assumption of top responsibility by
Clevelanders on the national level. Particularly during the second half of the thirty-
year period covered in this narrative, a substantial number of organizations were headed
by Clevelanders: United Jewish Appeal
(Edward Ginsberg), the Council of Jewish
Federations and Welfare Funds (Irving Kane),

Large City Budgeting Conference (Lawrence H. Williams), National Jewish Welfare Board (Morton L. Mandel), Joint Distribution Committee (Edward Ginsberg), American Jewish Congress (Rabbi Arthur J. Lelyveld), National Foundation for Jewish Culture (Rabbi Daniel J. Silver), National Jewish Community Relations Advisory Council (Irving Kane, Jordan C. Band), National Jewish War Veterans (Bernard Direnfeld), National Conference of Jewish Communal Services (Sidney Z. Vincent), American Israel Public Affairs Committee (Irving Kane), American-Israel Chamber of Commerce (Max Ratner), Jewish Occupational Council (Sidney Simon), Central Conference of American Rabbis (Rabbis Barnett R. Brickner and Arthur J. Lelyveld), American Jewish League for Israel (Ezra Z. Shapiro).

Cleveland was illustrating a maturing process typical of the American Jewish community as a whole—reaching beyond parochial concerns to forge mechanisms for dealing with the overwhelming national and international problems that affected all communities. The phrase "Never Again," which became a sometimes irresponsible slogan, nevertheless accurately reflected the temperament of the community in the postwar period as well as its new determination to shape its own history. It was one thing to be concerned primarily with local problems of health and welfare, as in the prewar period; it was quite different to assume the task of raising hundreds of millions of dollars, to plunge into the welter of events leading to the establishment of a state, to fight for the rights of Soviet Jewry, and to combat the rising tide of a new anti-Semitism throughout the world as symbolized in the United Nations resolution equating Zionism and racism.

The changes in attitude and involvement were reflected in the methods used for combating anti-Semitism. Before and during the Second World War a "front" organization, the League for Human Rights, was created in Cleveland to coordinate local efforts to boycott and otherwise resist Nazi Germany. Formation of such façades was common in those days, when it was considered inappropriate for a Jewish community to plead its own cause. As the years went on, such techniques were discarded. The community in its own name and through its own organizations vigorously petitioned for the formation of the state of Israel, for civil rights, and against Soviet tyranny.

Another indication of the growth in the complexity and breadth of the community's activities can be seen by comparing its response to two disastrous floods. In 1912 the response to an appeal for help for those suffering from the destructive Dayton flood was perhaps the outstanding piece of communal business for that year. Sixty years later another flood did major damage, this time to the Jewish community of Wilkes-Barre, Pennsylvania. The response was quick, efficient, and part of a coordinated national undertaking. Cleveland contributed $85,000 from communal funds as its assigned share. The grant constituted but one item on a full and complicated monthly meeting agenda.

A by-product of meeting challenges of growing dimensions was the increasing development of a sense of unity. With some reservations and modifications to be noted below, the traditional divisions in the community tended to diminish as the problems and threats (and Jewish opportunities) mounted. When support of Israel or of Soviet Jewry was the issue, the existence of Reform, Conservative, and Orthodox groupings proved little more divisive than the earlier and now humorous *Litvak*, *Galitzianer*, and Hungarian distinctions. Affluence, or at least some degree of fiscal ease, made former class divisions increasingly anachronistic; the outstanding leaders of the community were recent East European arrivals like Leonard Ratner or graduates of the Jewish Orphan Home (now

34 Bellefaire) like Maurice Saltzman, just as often
as they were descendants of old settlers.
A coherent community was being forged
out of the imperatives of world events and
concerns.

Merger of the Jewish Welfare Federation and the Jewish Community Council

Every Jewish institution felt the impact of
this heightened pulse of Jewish living—none
more than the Jewish Community Federation,
which, as one wag put it, increasingly ran
"the best show in town." It dispatched mis-
sions to Israel, where they were addressed by
the most charismatic personalities in the country; it conducted campaigns of unheard-of
dimensions; it sponsored meetings to con-
sider dramatic happenings overseas. This
ambitious program cost the organization some
popularity, however; it came to be regarded
in some quarters as a closed establishment,
accessible and responsive only at campaign
time. Such a view was hotly denied by representatives of the Federation, who pointed to
its continuing efforts to broaden its base
of representativeness; these included "Open
Door" programs, leadership development
sessions, establishment of an information and
referral service, and the continued existence of
a Delegate Assembly that designated a dozen
members of the Board of Trustees. Nevertheless, charges and countercharges about
"elitism" and "democracy" were frequently
mounted during the negotiations that even-
tually led to the merger of the Federation and
the Jewish Community Council in 1951 to
form the present Jewish Community Federation.

The Jewish Welfare Federation had created
the Council in 1935, partly as a response to
the growing demands for "democratization"
at that time. The chief means employed to

secure a democratic base was the creation of
a Delegate Assembly as the authoritative body
of the Council. It was in part composed of a representative of every organization in the community having a membership of at least
seventy-five and a "legitimate Jewish purpose." That definition at times led to unforeseen complications. In 1950 the Council found
itself involved in a serious schism as a result
of a nationwide investigation of one of its
constituent organizations, the Jewish
People's Fraternal Order. The charge was that
this organization's fundamental national purpose was determined by Communist, not Jewish, objectives, but the local delegate and
chapter had been faithful both in attendance
and in support of Council objectives. Should
it continue to remain part of the Council?
Did it serve a "legitimate Jewish purpose?"
The debate on this issue formed one of the
most vivid chapters of Council history and
finally resulted in the expulsion of the JPFO
from the Council. The issue was not settled,
however, and debate continued as to whether the
Council had yielded to the "McCarthyism" of
the period or had conducted itself with intel-
ligence and sophistication.

At any rate, during its fifteen-year history
the Council outgrew its original program,
which was primarily limited to community relations, the fight against anti-Semitism, and
Jewish cultural projects—all activities
involving no jurisdictional questions—and
increasingly became involved in broader
questions of community planning and policy.
These were matters that were the direct
concern of the Federation. The need for
clarifying the respective roles of the two organizations came to a head when communities throughout the country were asked in
the forties to define their position on an
appropriate division of funds raised by the
United Jewish Appeal between its two major
beneficiaries—the Joint Distribution Com-

Rabbi Abba Hillel Silver addressing the United Nations on behalf of a Jewish state; with him are Moshe Sharett and Golda Meir. 1947 (The Temple)

36 mittee and the United Israel Appeal.
Feelings ran high everywhere on the issue
of the equitable division of funds between
relief needs in Europe and the costs of
immigration into and absorption in Israel. In
Cleveland there was the further question of
which organizational judgment should pre-
vail. The disagreement climaxed a series of al-
tercations that had left both agencies feeling
aggrieved—the Council, that its allegedly
more democratic and popular views were
being overlooked; the Federation, that
the Council, its own creation, was exceeding
its mandate and moving into areas where its
work would inevitably be duplicative and
where in any case it could not perform effectively or, some felt, responsibly.

It was only natural that the idea of merger
should arise. In the prolonged negotiations
that followed, the real issue was the representativeness and democracy of the community. Breakdown threatened on a number
of occasions up to the last minute, when a
deadlock arose over the name of the new organization. A compromise was finally reached
with the agreement on "Jewish Community
Federation," which not only combined elements of the names of both organizations but
effectively described the direction to be
taken by the combined organization—toward
emphasis on overall community needs
rather than concern with "welfare" alone.

Agreement did not come easily. The meeting
of the Council's Delegate Assembly that finally approved merger did so by a single
vote and after impassioned speeches in
English and Yiddish to the effect that the
"democratic" partner would be swallowed up.
Doubts on the Federation side were expressed less dramatically but no less strongly.
The agreement was reached largely because
the leaders of both organizations were extraordinarily patient men who were closely involved with the operation of both agencies.
Henry Rocker, Federation president (subse-

quently to be elected first president of the
combined agency), was the son of Samuel
Rocker, founder of the *Yiddishe Velt* and for
years a venerated symbol of democracy in
the community. He himself was the perfect
compromiser—quiet-spoken, modest, fair,
infinitely patient. Jerome Curtis and Irving
Kane, presidents of the Council during the
years of negotiation, were simultaneously
deeply involved in Federation affairs as well
as nationally prominent in the CJF. As already
noted, Max Simon, first president of the
Council, subsequently became president of
the Federation, the only person to serve both
organizations in that role.

The agencies and their staffs merged in
1951, but nostalgia for the past continued to be
expressed for years afterward and only gradually subsided as the new organization demonstrated its effectiveness and increasing openness to all sections of the community. The
final act in this drama of democratic combination did not take place until 1968, when
Ezra Shapiro, a former president of the
Council, requested permission to second the
nomination of William C. Treuhaft as an
honorary trustee of the Federation. At the
time of merger many had perceived these men
as symbolizing the two contrasting organizations—one a grass roots group oriented to
Yiddishkeit and Israel, the other oriented to
health and welfare and the necessity of raising adequate funds. Over the years both per-
ceptions proved to be far too glib: Shapiro
became head of a worldwide fund-raising
agency, and Treuhaft electrified the community at the time of the Six-Day War by
calling for a million-dollar Endowment Fund
gift and vigorously backing every campaign toward promoting Jewish commitment and broadening the base of participation in communal undertakings. The merger
of the two agencies and all it represented as a
symbol of communal unity was therefore
finally achieved in spirit almost twenty

1.

2.

3.

1.   Charles de Harrack emigrated to Cleveland as a child in the early 1890s. He began his musical studies in Cleveland and continued them in Berlin and Vienna. After performing in Europe, he returned to Cleveland after the outbreak of World War I. Until his retirement he was active as a performer, composer, teacher and choral director; he served as director of the Cleveland Jewish Singing Society 1921–1929. Vienna, ca. 1909 (Charles de Harrack)

2.   Maurice Goldman, born in Cleveland and trained at the Institute of Music, was prominent in classical and Jewish musical circles as a singer and composer until he left to continue his career in Hollywood. He returned in 1954 as composer of the cantata, "The Golden Door," script by Norman Corwin, which highlighted Cleveland's celebration of the tercentenary of Jewish settlement in the United States. ca. 1954 (Cleveland *Jewish News*)

3.   Victor Babin, internationally known pianist and composer, came to Cleveland in 1961 as director of the Cleveland Institute of Music, serving until his death in 1972. He is shown here with three distinguished Cleveland musicians, Ernst Silberstein, cello; Abraham Skernick, viola; and Dr. Jerome Gross, violin. March 29, 1968 (Cleveland Institute of Music)

38 years after the amalgamation had been formally completed.

Role of Women

Four years after the merger of the Federation and the Community Council, the Federation of Jewish Women's Organizations (FJWO), which had been in existence since 1921 as the overall coordinating mechanism for women's organizations, was also incorporated within the Jewish Community Federation and was renamed the Women's Organization (WO). In 1974 after considerable self-study, the WO was again reconstituted, this time as the Women's Committee of Federation. More than the name was changed; conscious attempt was made to structure the new committee in such a way as to parallel all other Federation standing committees. Each of these changes reflected shifts in the way women defined their role in the community—always in the direction of greater involvement in the mainstreams of community life and away from isolation or insularity as "just (or only) women's" organizations. Some sentiment was expressed for eliminating a separate women's organization and instead working for fully integrated representation by women in every phase of communal activity. It was claimed in support of this thesis that the very existence of a separate women's organization inevitably led to segregation because talented women were "assigned out" to women's concerns. The majority felt, however, that at least for the time being it was more effective to secure more WO designees on key Federation activities (Board of Trustees, Endowment Fund, Budget, and Planning Committees) than to have the WO go out of business. The realities seemed to be that separate and distinctive activities for women and women's organizations continued to be a feature of communal life and therefore validated separate representation on various organizations.

Although women served on virtually every Board of Trustees and every major committee of almost every organization in the city, top leadership of most Jewish organizations remained largely male. Mrs. Hilda Faigin was elected vice president of Fairmount Temple, but no woman had ever served in the top post of any congregation. Among the agencies, only the Jewish Family Service Association could claim that women played a major role in its leadership; four of its presidents during the postwar period (Mrs. Rosalie Udelf, Mrs. Anne Miller, Mrs. Florence Arsham, and Dr. Sally Wertheim) were women. The Jewish Vocational Service (Mrs. Frieda Yoelson), the Jewish Community Center (Mrs. Hilda Faigin), and Hillel (Mrs. Elaine Rocker) also had women presidents, but men continued to occupy most top positions. Typically, one office was "reserved" for a woman in most organizations, but she rarely progressed to the presidency. On the professional level, only one organization, the Jewish Family Service Association, had a woman chief executive (Mrs. Rae Weil).

Reference has already been made to the vigor of the women's Zionist organizations in contrast to the men's groups. Evidently tangible tasks such as undertaking projects, assigning quotas, and arranging "donors" made for more involvement than did generalized programs. Certainly the women sometimes developed elaborate ongoing programs of education that went beyond the bread and butter work of raising funds but, equally certainly, fund-raising usually provided the essential base for organizational vitality.

One of the largest and most prestigious women's organizations was the Council of Jewish Women, with a record of service to the community dating back to before the turn of

THE CLEVELAND ORCHESTRA

GEORGE SZELL, *Conductor*

SIXTH PROGRAM

THURSDAY EVENING, NOVEMBER 18, 1948, *at 8:30 O'clock*
SATURDAY EVENING, NOVEMBER 20, 1948, *at 8:30 O'clock*

ARTHUR LOESSER, *Piano*

Overture to "Oberon"   Weber

"Kenaan"   Berlinski
    (Winning score in the Jewish Music Contest sponsored by the Music Committee of the Cleveland Jewish Community Council in coöperation with the National Jewish Musical Council. First performance.)

Concerto for Piano and Orchestra No. 1 in C major,   Beethoven
  Op. 15

    Allegro con brio (Cadenza by Beethoven)
    Largo
    Rondo: Allegro
        (First performance at these concerts)

INTERMISSION

Symphony No. 4 in D minor, Op. 120   Schumann

    Andante; Allegro
    Romanza
    Scherzo
    Finale: Largo; Allegro
        Played without pause

Mr. Loesser uses the Steinway
The Steinway is the official piano of the Cleveland Orchestra
The Cleveland Orchestra records exclusively for Columbia

169

1. Cleveland Orchestra premiere of Jacques Berlinski's "Kenaan," prize winning score in Jewish Community Council national music contest. 1948 (Jewish Community Federation)

2. The Eisenman Award presented to Mr. and Mrs. William C. Treuhaft for a career of distinguished community service at the 47th Annual Meeting of the Jewish Community Federation. Pictured are Mr. Treuhaft, Mrs. Sigmund Herzog, Nathan Loeser, Mrs. Treuhaft and Edward Baker. 1950 (Jewish Community Federation)

3. I. F. Freiberger (center) with Mayor Anthony J. Celebrezze and Senator Thomas A. Burke at the 50th Annual Meeting of the Jewish Community Federation. 1953 (Jewish Community Federation)

Women's Division campaigners, Jewish Welfare Fund. 1951 (Jewish Community Federation)

the century. Its extensive volunteer activities, its thrift shops—also sponsored, among other organizations, by Hadassah, Women's ORT (Organization for Rehabilitation and Training), and Pioneer Women—its legislative seminars, and its cultural programs were outgrowths of activities initiated decades earlier. Perhaps its most outstanding accomplishment was the creation in 1958 of Council Gardens, a housing project for the well aged, on Taylor Road. It was an immediate success and thereafter continued to meet a need for modest housing for the independent elderly. Both its lay and its professional heads left the stamp of their personalities on the project: Mrs. Ruth Einstein was in her late seventies when she gave vigorous and cheerful leadership to the new idea and lived into her nineties to enjoy its fruition; and Al Brown was the project's tireless director from its founding until his retirement in 1975, bringing to the job all the energy and enthusiasm he had demonstrated decades earlier as director of Camp Wise, the communal summer camp.

Other traditional women's organizations included the sisterhoods of congregations, the Mt. Sinai Auxiliaries, and the B'nai B'rith Women's chapters. To this list new groups were added during the postwar period, notably the very active Women's ORT and the Brandeis University Women's Organization. All provided programs and activities for burgeoning memberships.

Despite the proliferation of these organized activities, women's liberation–not as a formal movement but as a mood and impulse–may well have had more impact on women's roles than traditional organization structures. Many women whose children had grown up turned to professional tasks, part-time and full-time, within and outside the Jewish community, rather than limiting their options for expression and involvement to organiza-

tional work. Mrs. Rena Blumberg became the first woman to be elected an officer of the City Club, which for most of its history had been limited to men; Dr. Ruth Miller became public health director and then community development director in the cabinet of Mayor Ralph J. Perk, another first for Jewish women; the communications and public relations industries attracted increasing numbers of Jewish women, notably the redoubtable Dorothy Fuldheim, who as an octogenarian could look back on a career of more than thirty years, making her the most senior news commentator in the country. No longer were women limited to working as teachers, librarians, social workers, or stenographers; nor did starting a family preclude a career.

Role of Youth

How to appraise the commitment of Jewish youth in the postwar period was a question calculated to start major debates between those who "viewed with alarm" and those who "pointed with pride." The former claimed that young people were drifting away from Jewish life, citing national statistics to prove it; the national rate of intermarriage was approaching fifty percent, and there was no reason to suppose that the situation in Cleveland was much different. They argued vociferously that assimilation was inherent in a situation where Jewish and non-Jewish children were viewing the same television programs, playing the same sports, singing the same songs, and dancing the same dances. The openness of typically liberal parents was often perceived by their children as a rationale to mingle and to date and to marry whomever romantic impulses dictated.

But there was considerable evidence pointing toward a strong reaction. Jewish studies courses at the university level, hitherto an unknown phenomenon in Cleveland, were intro-

1.

2.

3.

1. Dedicating memorial at the Jewish Community Center to David Berger, victim of the 1972 Munich Olympic massacre; with Senator Howard Metzenbaum, Senator Hubert H. Humphrey and Dr. and Mrs. Benjamin Berger. 1974 (Jewish Community Center)

2. The Tercentenary program celebrating three-hundred years of Jewish life in America. 1955 (Jewish Community Federation)

3. Starting the addition to the Heights Jewish Center with Rabbi Israel Porath and Rabbi Emeritus Ozer Palay in 1947. (Heights Jewish Center)

duced on virtually every college campus in the area. At Case Western Reserve University, where the Abba Hillel Silver Chair in Jewish Studies was established in 1962, and at Oberlin, Jewish studies could be taken as a major. In both cases, the programs resulted from joint planning and financing by the Federation and the universities. (The Silver Chair was financed by the Federation, the Cleveland Foundation, and the Beaumont Foundation.) Also with the cooperation of the Federation, Hebrew House was established at Oberlin in 1970 and continued to attract live-in students year after year. Even colleges established under Christian sectarian auspices, like John Carroll, Hiram, and Baldwin Wallace, added programs of Jewish interest.

New ground was broken at Kent State University when the communities of Canton, Akron, and Youngstown joined with Cleveland in establishing and subsidizing a Hillel program; it received the active support of Jewish faculty members, who helped devise a series of offerings in Judaica. The Hillel operation was radically transformed from a one-college organization at Case Western Reserve University to a regional structure serving seven campuses with a greatly expanded program. Increased subvention came from the community as the traditional support from B'nai B'rith proved incapable of meeting the costs of the expanded programs.

If Jewish students of the sixties played a leading role in movements aimed at ameliorating social and political conditions in the general community, their successors in the seventies were concerned with international events affecting Jewry and with new means of strengthening Jewish life at home. The continuing campaign for the rights of Soviet Jews drew some of its strongest support from the local campuses; protest meetings in reaction to United Nations actions hostile to Israel regularly turned out the blue-jean crowd; when

the Yom Kippur War broke out, young volunteers eager to go to Israel's defense swamped local offices they felt could help them get to the Middle East. After college demonstrators in Boston at the 1969 General Assembly of the CJF demanded that communities give greater priority to Jewish commitment programs, a number of local activities were initiated, including the establishment of a local *Havura* (a commune for Jewish fellowship), the proliferation of courses in Judaica and exchange visits to Israel, and the publication of a monthly newspaper, *Hashofar*. A group of young leaders on the Case Western Reserve campus helped create the national organization called "Network," which acted as an umbrella for five self-created and self-run Jewish youth organizations seeking the reinvigoration of Jewish life (and, not so incidentally, some funding from federations, which were viewed as a kind of friendly enemy). "Walkathons" that raised money for overseas needs and the activities of the Youth Division of the Welfare Fund touched the lives of thousands of young Jews. So did the many youth programs sponsored by the Jewish Community Center, the congregations, the Chabad movement, and B'nai B'rith.

No easy generalizations can adequately characterize Cleveland (or American) Jewish youth of the postwar period. There was substantial intermarriage,[16] as well as skepticism about "The Establishment"—a term which could include synagogues and the Federation and its agencies. Membership and participation in traditional Jewish activities were erratic. But there was also little doubt that Jewish young people were strongly committed to Israel despite the Third World hostility that shaped the attitudes of so many of their liberal non-Jewish counterparts. Nor was there any doubt of their determination to have a say ("input" was the preferred word) in the de-

Internal Developments

1.

2.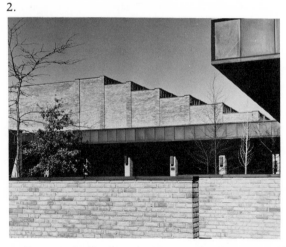

3.

1. Bringing the Torah to the Marmarosher Synagogue, Cleveland Heights. 1958 (Western Reserve Historical Society)

2. The Temple Branch, Pepper Pike; architects Perkins & Will, Chicago; dedicated 1970. (The Temple)

3. Brith Emeth, Pepper Pike; architect Edward Durell Stone; dedicated 1968. 1975 (Richard E. Karberg)

velopment of Jewish life in the next generation.

Role of Agencies

This same drive toward increased Jewish commitment affected the twenty-three agencies serving the community.[17] Their general growth during the three decades was reflected in their budgets. Excluding Mt. Sinai Hospital, whose annual budget by the mid-seventies reached $37,000,000, the combined budgets of the other agencies rose from $2,000,000 in 1946 to $6,000,000 in 1966 and to $13,000,000 in 1976.

This escalation, which considerably outpaced the general rise in costs for the period, reflected greatly expanded services, since the agencies were increasingly called on to serve all members of the community, not only the underprivileged. The Jewish Vocational Service counselled the sons and daughters of some of the "best" families, as well as trying to find jobs for the Jewish handicapped; the homes for the aged, shifting their emphasis from care of the well aged to care of those no longer able to be looked after in their own homes, were deluged by applicants from all sectors of the community; the Jewish Family Service Association and Bellefaire dealt with the problems of the affluent as well as the hard pressed. It was a long way from the immigrant days, when the agencies were primarily mechanisms for Americanizing the "greenhorns," and when the community was basically divided between "givers" and "takers."

The agency that perhaps best illustrated the change in emphasis was the Jewish Community Center (JCC). Even the name was new, having been adopted in 1948 when a lengthy Group Work Study concluded with a recommendation that the Council Educational Alliance, the Jewish Young Adult Bureau, the Cultural Department of the Jewish Community Council, and Camp Wise be merged into a single agency. It was a merger not only of institutions but of interests. Camp Wise in particular was a classic illustration of the transition to universal service. It had been established in 1907 as a fresh-air camp to bring two weeks of nature and the outdoors to poor and underprivileged children and mothers. Fees charged were nominal and often waived altogether. By 1975, in contrast, most of the campers paid full per capita cost, and the constituency reflected a broad spectrum of the community, while the program's educational objectives were undistinguishable from those of many private camps, except for the major emphasis on Jewish content.

The JCC emerged almost simultaneously with the publication nationally by the National Jewish Welfare Board of the influential Janowsky Report, with its major recommendation that Jewish community centers place increased emphasis on their Jewish programming. The Cleveland JCC was quick to respond. The Group Work Study, in its section on the role of the camp, stated that it

should shift away from a "charity" service for underprivileged to a group work program with positive Jewish aims. The agency . . . is created by the Jewish community to offer vital group experience to Jewish children and youth. The object of this experience should be the adjustment of Jewish youth to their own group, to its cultural, ethical and religious backgrounds, and to its community affairs, as well as the adjustment of young people to general American life.[18]

The same emphasis spread throughout the agency. A drama department was created that stressed the Jewish heritage; the Yiddish Cultural Committee nurtured the linguistic riches of Yiddish; a full time *shaliach* (Israeli representative) was employed to foster relationships with Israel; the yearly calendar of events of the agency emphasized observances of the Warsaw Ghetto uprising and the birth of the State of Israel; participation in "Jewish happenings" was a constant agency concern.

Involvement of recipients of service in decision-making, a goal that would become dominant in the thinking of the social welfare programs of the general community a decade later, was defined as an objective in the annual report of 1950, the second year of the agency's operation:

Democratic participation in program and policy making reached a high level with over 400 persons participating in various advisory committees. . . . A long range plan for giving basic training in community leadership has been evolved.[19]

Paradoxically, while the broadening of lay participation in agency affairs was adopted as a key objective in most agencies, the professionalization of their services was simultaneously completed. The procedure at many of the agencies was that volunteers provided services to clients. The tradition of *"noblesse oblige"*— that it was obligatory to devote part of one's time to such projects as serving as a leader at the summer camp—no longer prevailed. It had ended, as far as the camp was concerned, as a result of the economic realities of the Second World War. In 1936 Albert Kinoy, once an assistant director at the Council Educational Alliance and later director of Camp Wise, had stated: "One can't base all work on professional social work. . . . The effervescence of the volunteer is as necessary as the finished product and outlook of the professional worker."[20] But thirteen years later another staff member, Irwin Gold, reported that "despite the fact that summer jobs are few and far between, we find that young people as a rule no longer want to volunteer their services at camp." The role of the volunteer would continue to be invaluable, but primarily in setting policy and in providing aid to the professional staff rather than in assuming full functional responsibility.

The Jewish Family Service Association, whose year-long centennial observance in 1975 provided an opportunity for the community to review the agency's accomplishments during the century, broadened its mandate in a number of directions in response to new influences affecting and eroding family life. Its project known as RapArt, launched together with the Jewish Community Center, sought to counsel and guide alienated young people caught up or tempted by the drug culture. Such a project would never have occurred to earlier generations. The incidence of delinquency and family breakdown had for decades been significantly lower in the Jewish than in the general community; as late as 1943, a community study revealed that barely one percent of the total delinquent population was Jewish, though Jews then constituted five percent of the total community. But as the immigrant generation passed from the scene, the pace of acculturation increased, and the values of the general society were reflected in a higher incidence of divorce, problems with drugs, and other signs of malaise affecting society as a whole. Interestingly, the agency reported no significant increase in alcoholism.

At the same time as the agency sought to adapt its services to new conditions, however, it was also required to return to one of its oldest and most traditional activities. Three times during the postwar period major eruptions overseas resulted in the agency's caring for waves of new immigrants as it had done early in its history, but with a difference.

The uprising and subsequent harsh suppression of the Freedom Fighters in Hungary in 1956 brought hundreds of immigrant families to Cleveland, some of them Jewish, but the newcomers differed from earlier immigrants. Many brought with them the passions and hatreds of the Nazi period and were patronizing and contemptuous in their attitude

1.

2.

1. Israel Emergency Fund Rally during the Six Day War at the Hotel Cleveland. 1967 (Jewish Community Federation)

2. The Jewish Community Center, Cleveland Heights; architects Sigmund Braverman and Moses Halperin; facade sculpture by William McVey; dedicated 1959. (Berni Rich)

1.

2.

3.

1. Celebration of Israel's tenth anniversary at Severance Hall. 1958 (Jewish Community Federation)

2. Cleveland Youth Walk-a-Thon after Ma'alot, Israel, attack. 1974 (Jewish Community Federation)

3. A Soviet Jewish father and daughter celebrate Passover in Cleveland. 1975 (Jewish Family Service Association)

toward the older Hungarian settlers, who were less cultured, less political, and more liberal and easygoing. For a short time Cleveland again experienced the threats of an anti-Semitism more typical of the thirties, until the normal process of acculturation weakened the movement.

The flight from Cuba following the triumph of Castro added only a handful of Jewish Cuban families, among them Dr. Josef Edelstein, destined to become one of Cleveland's leading cardiologists as well as an active participant in Jewish communal affairs.

The partial and erratic lifting of barriers to emigration from Soviet Russia in the early seventies presented far more complex problems. Although the numbers were still relatively modest (143 arrived in Cleveland in 1975), the adjustment to life in an open society was difficult, particularly because so many of the new arrivals had skills not easily utilized in the West. Teachers of Russian literature or "engineers" or medical personnel whose credentials were unacceptable understandably resented having to work, when jobs could be found, at less professional levels. To fight against Russian tyranny was brutal but ennobling; to struggle with the jawbreaking English language or bewildering (and bewildered) employers was frustrating. Never in Cleveland's history had immigrants been so planned for or cared for. Representatives of the Jewish Family Service Association met them at the plane, arranged housing, and accepted financial responsibility; the Jewish Vocational Service found them jobs; the Jewish Community Center offered courses in English and extended services; Mt. Sinai Hospital was concerned about their health; and the Jewish Community Federation paid most of the bills for these services, while a whole host of voluntary organizations undertook other responsibilities.

Also active was Chabad, relatively new to the Cleveland scene but intensely interested in the "Jewish absorption" of the Soviet immigrants as part of their vigorous program of urging greater Jewish depth in all aspects of Jewish life. The fact that substantial problems of adjustment still remained, including the complex question of their relation with Judaism, attested to the vast changes that had taken place in the century between the first massive wave of immigration to Cleveland and the arrival of these sophisticated urban newcomers, with their high expectations and demands.

Those changes were sometimes characterized as a transition from "making Americans out of Jews" to "making Jews out of new Americans." Those who came streaming in by the thousands at the turn of the century had been totally at home in the traditions of Jewish life; many of the new immigrants from the Soviet Union hardly knew the names of the Jewish holidays. The JFSA had for generations provided expert guidance on adjustment to American life; now it was asked to perform the same function in building relationships to Jewish life.

This increasing emphasis on Jewish credentials affected all the agencies. Their specifically Jewish performance was a matter not only of ideology, but also of pragmatism. As the quality and costs of services rendered by the Jewish agencies continued to rise, and as many of them served the non-Jewish community in increasing degree, the question whether the Jewish community could or should continue to support them grew more insistent.

Mt. Sinai Hospital grew dramatically after the war, becoming one of the four major hospitals serving the general community. It was located closest to the Hough neighborhood, which became in the postwar period both completely black and one of the most underprivileged sections of the city. Its out-

1.

2.

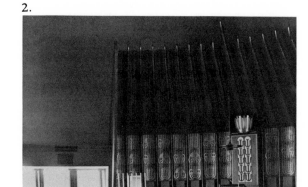

3.

4.

1. Park Synagogue, Cleveland Heights; architect Eric Mendelsohn; dedicated 1951. 1967 (Albert Willinger)

2. Sanctuary, Park Synagogue. 1975 (Richard E. Karberg)

3. Fairmount Temple, Beachwood; architect Percival Goodman; dedicated 1957. 1975 (Richard E. Karberg)

4. Sanctuary, Fairmount Temple. 1975 (Richard E. Karberg)

patient department clientele became overwhelmingly non-Jewish, and even its overnight clientele became approximately only half Jewish. Should the hospital move to a more Jewish neighborhood? What was Jewish about its services?

Bellefaire became recognized throughout the country as one of a limited number of institutions equipped to deal in depth with the growing problem of disturbed youngsters, but half of its residents were not Jewish. Could its Jewish purpose be preserved regardless of the makeup of its clientele?

The homes for the aged presented a different problem. Both Montefiore Home and Menorah Park (formerly the Jewish Orthodox Home for the Aged, now located in a superb new building at the far eastern edge of the community) not only rendered outstanding service in a field where the general community had failed to meet its responsibilities, but also provided much of the state leadership in the movement to raise standards for care of the elderly. Howard Bram, director of Menorah Park, and Sidney Lewine, director of Mt. Sinai Hospital, were elected presidents of state associations in their fields and contributed in major ways to setting health and welfare standards; David N. Myers was the chief inspiration for the dramatic rise of Menorah Park to its position as an outstanding institution for care of the elderly.

Both institutions for the aged served an exclusively Jewish clientele on the thesis that they were indeed "homes"; it therefore became necessary to explain continually that this situation derived from their responsibility for meeting religious as well as health needs. Third-party payments had become so basic an aspect of their support that it seemed certain that the question of their Jewish separateness (and that of the other Jewish agencies depending on such support) would continue to be raised. The dramatic growth of the

civil rights movement, insisting on a prime responsibility of publicly supported services to the underprivileged, would see to that.

As early as 1945 the Welfare Federation of Cleveland "urged all Boards . . . and Agencies to make a statement of principle . . . and to do everything possible to aid in the promulgation of good race relations. We request the abandonment of a policy of service for one race or group exclusively. The purpose of all agencies at this time should be to serve all races."[21] That rather simple statement was subsequently followed by both governmental agencies and the United Way (later called the United Torch Services, UTS) when they sought to determine whether a policy of nondiscrimination had actually been adopted.

All the affected Jewish agencies repeatedly submitted evidence that they served the total community in many ways, and that they were in theory and in practice strongly opposed to any form of racial discrimination. At the same time, they added that they were sectarian organizations existing to fulfill a specifically Jewish purpose, and they were therefore required to implement that objective by adopting a Jewish program. Their services were available without discrimination to those accepting that commitment. Their position was succinctly expressed at one Board meeting:

As a Jewish agency, we can continue to defend our separateness only in that we have a specific Jewish function to fulfill, as our program shows. A definition of [our] philosophy and purpose and aims must be clearly stated.[22]

The need to interpret the rationale for separate Jewish agencies was never-ending. The relationship of the United Way with the Jewish agencies had always been cordial, as exemplified concretely by the fact that almost half the subvention of those agencies (excluding Mt. Sinai Hospital) was through

1.

2.

1. The Jewish Community Federation; Edward Durell Stone and Weinberg and Teare, associated architects; dedicated 1965. (Albert Willinger)

2. The building under construction. Standing in the girders are M.E. Glass, Joseph M. Berne and Henry L. Zucker. 1964 (Jewish Community Federation)

support from the annual United Way campaign. (The other half of their annual budget deficit came from the Jewish Welfare Fund.) Upon the reorganization of the UTS in 1971, the entire question of the relationship of the fund-raising arm of the general community to the Jewish agencies was again explored. The resulting policy agreement restated the mutual responsibilities of the Federation and the UTS and recognized the validity of the specifically sectarian purposes of the Jewish agencies. It was, however, a policy arrived at by leadership; the general community did not always understand or fully accept the Jewish distinctiveness of the agencies. Since the services extended by the Jewish agencies were widely recognized as outstanding (and in many cases more costly than less adequate services generally available), it was necessary for these agencies constantly to reiterate their position that the community should seek to raise standards for all its agencies rather than to lower the Jewish agency services to the lowest common communal denominator.

The insistence on preserving cultural distinctiveness, reversing the earlier melting pot assumptions, found support in other ethnic groups, even while some critics were simultaneously finding it hard to accept the validity of a separate Jewish service function. Vernon Jordan, Jr., executive director of the National Urban League, put the case for the distinctiveness of black institutions and, by inference, of sectarian institutions as well:

It is . . . important, both for our pluralistic society as a whole and for its educational system, that key institutions serving the minority community and providing it with leadership and with opportunities, preserve much of their character and cultural orientation. . . .

At issue is not the concept of integration, but the way in which it is carried out. Thus, black citizens will be vigilant in assuring that integration does not become synonymous with the destruction of historic black institutions. It cannot be allowed to become the vehicle for the dismantling of black community strengths. True integration should mean the preservation of those institutional strengths in altered, modernized forms that allow those traditionally black institutions to use their history of expertise and their unique resources to serve the total community.[23]

Jewish Education

One field that obviously had no need to prove its Jewish credentials, at least theoretically, was Jewish education. In Cleveland, as throughout the nation, it was this community activity that received the most communal dollars and caused the most concern. This paralleled the situation in the general community, where problems of education also moved front and center with comparable challenges and frustrations. If the general community grew worried that Johnnie couldn't read and wasn't interested in being able to write (or even spell), the Jewish community was worried about what it felt was the growing Jewish illiteracy of the upcoming generation. Meanwhile, costs escalated dramatically; the subvention in Cleveland for Jewish education for the communal schools (excluding the congregations) grew from $75,729 in 1945 to $1,085,924 in 1975, far exceeding the rise in other fields. The cost of education to congregations, where the majority of the children were educated, grew correspondingly. But the payoff was not clearly apparent. Although by far the largest part of the increase went for salaries, outstanding teachers remained hard to get; yet they were perhaps even more crucial to Jewish than to general schools, since attendance of students was voluntary (except for parental pressures, which often could not stand up against the child's resistance). The continuing

54 concern with the schools was reflected in the fact that three major studies of Jewish education were undertaken, in 1954, 1964, and 1974. Though each resulted in substantial changes and improvements, there was an uneasy feeling that, with the exception of the all-day schools, formal education could not possibly accomplish what the combination of vigorous Jewish family life and a coherent, all-pervasive Jewish community had done for earlier generations facing fewer distractions, with more limited alternatives.

The creation of whole new educational institutions was another vivid illustration of the importance attached to the schools. In fields other than education not a single new communal institution was created in the thirty-year period from 1945 to 1975, although the existing organizations' names, locations, and functions were changed and expanded. In education, on the other hand, the field proliferated. In 1945 the Federation supported two afternoon Hebrew schools (the Cleveland Hebrew Schools and Yeshivath Adath B'nai Israel), a Sunday school (United Jewish Religious Schools), and a Yiddishist school (the Workmen's Circle School). In the next thirty years, it added two all-day schools—the Hebrew Academy, a traditional Orthodox school, and Agnon School, a liberal institution; Akiva, a communal high school; and a College of Jewish Studies. In addition, the Montessori School, under the auspices of Park Synagogue, and several smaller private schools with basically secularist goals also attested to the Jewish desire to tackle and solve the problem of passing on the heritage.

The record of the day schools was particularly significant. Founded as the war was ending, with only a handful of students, the Hebrew Academy quickly expanded until by the mid-seventies it was conducting a full educational program for over six hundred students from kindergarten through high school. Equally impressive was its ability to retain its student body. Almost every school, public or private, declined dramatically in enrollment in the decade 1965–1975, as the products of the earlier postwar baby boom passed out of the school system, to be succeeded by fewer children born in the age of the pill and zero population growth. Hebrew Academy alone did not lose students, a testament either to its tenacious and vigorous director for thirty years, Rabbi Nahum Dessler, or to the increasing appeal of intensive Jewish education, or both. Certainly its hold on its constituents could not be ascribed to permissive methods or to absorption in being "relevant" to student needs by adapting subject matter to satisfy youthful interests. Its own interpretation of relevance was that students need the teachings prescribed by tradition, and its demands were rigorous: six days of classes, long hours, a long school year, and full curricula in both Judaic and general studies.

The other day school, Agnon, was founded in 1970 with the aim of providing parents with a liberal all-day alternative, utilizing progressive educational ideas and integrating Jewish and general studies rather than separating them as was the procedure at Hebrew Academy. It also grew, to approximately two hundred students by 1975, despite its lack of a building of its own and of continuing support like that provided to the Academy by Irving I. Stone, its long-time president and constant backer and fund-raiser, and his family.

The general attitude toward Jewish education, a mixture of hope and expectation coupled with adult disappointment and youthful rebellion, was reflected in the introductory comments in the report of the committee appointed in 1974 to study the field:

1.

2.

3.

4.

1.   William Rosenwald, Rabbi Abba Hillel Silver, and Rabbi Jonah B. Wise at founding of the United Jewish Appeal. 1938 (The Temple)

2.   Jewish Welfare Fund Campaign Opening with the Hon. Robert Briscoe, Lord Mayor of Dublin. 1957 (Jewish Community Federation)

3.   Ezra and Sylvia Shapiro with Golda Meir. 1952 (Jewish Community Federation)

4.   Irene Zehman, Eleanor Roosevelt, Charlotte Herman, and Isabel Brown. 1954 (Jewish Community Federation)

David Ben Gurion arrives in Cleveland. Seated with him, David N. Myers and Leonard Ratner; in front seat, Max Simon, Sam Friedman, Ben Blaushild; Suggs Garber stands at right. 1951 (Miriam Klein)

We have been warned by a number of the experts with whom we have consulted that 'romantic aspirations' for our work would inevitably cause disappointment to those reading the ensuing pages in the hope of finding there the authoritative answer to why their children or their grandchildren have been disappointed in their Jewish educational experience. We request that such disappointment be converted into joining us in assuming responsibility in further searching for many answers. . . .

We came to that conclusion because the aim of Jewish education is the transfer of values and commitment from generation to generation and that objective can best be accomplished through the united and complementary efforts of the schools, the family, the synagogues, and the community and its agencies. One of the major causes of the difficulties of Jewish education in modern times has been the tendency to assign responsibility for Jewish commitment exclusively to the schools, with little involvement of the other crucial partners in the educational process.[24]

Congregational Experience

Congregations, too, faced a period of change during the postwar years. Following the war, when the babies resulting from reunited families reached school age, congregational memberships boomed. Long-established congregations reached new heights in family membership, with each of the "Big Four" (The Temple, Fairmount Temple, Park Synagogue, and Temple on the Heights) approaching or exceeding the two thousand mark. In addition, the number of new congregations founded was unprecedented. Most were of substantial size almost from their founding, unlike the pattern of an earlier day, when modest beginnings, even store fronts, were the rule. Suburban Temple, Temple Emanu El, and B'rith Emeth not only had "instant" memberships numbering in the hundreds; each, after a brief period

of utilizing alternate facilities, was able to construct an impressive structure of its own.

In the Orthodox community mergers became common and resulted in congregations of substantial size, like Taylor Road Synagogue (900 members) and Warrensville Center Synagogue (700 members). The Young Israel movement, with approximately 350 members, provided the community with considerable dynamism that extended beyond its own membership.

The relationship of the Orthodox community to the general Jewish community was a checkered one. In 1947, reacting to the chaotic condition of the meat industry and the questionable practices among some of those involved in supplying kosher products, Orthodox Jews vigorously worked for a community-wide approach to the problem. In a model of determined and aggressive organization, they united with the Jewish Community Council in a massive approach to every kosher butcher and slaughter house, insistently pleading the case for submission to a city-wide inspection system. The result was the establishment of the Kashruth Board, administered by representatives of the Orthodox Rabbinical Council, the butchers, the slaughterers, and the community at large, and totally supported by communal funds. Thirty years later, it was still providing daily inspection of every kosher shop. A similar successful endeavor was the establishment of the Central Fund for Traditional Institutions, which sought, and substantially achieved, the elimination of innumerable *mishulochim* (solicitors) for traditional yeshivas and charitable organizations, mostly overseas, by combining their requests into a single annual campaign. The Kashruth Board and the Central Fund were viewed with great satisfaction by the Orthodox community as examples of what can be accomplished by careful organization and working within a community setting.

Orthodox institutions in general were generously supported: the Hebrew Academy's subvention was probably the largest in the country to any day school, while the Yeshivath Adath B'nai Israel, an Orthodox afternoon Hebrew school, was retained as an independent system despite a recommendation in 1954 to merge it with the Cleveland Hebrew Schools because its small size made it impractical to operate. The community demonstrated its respect for ideology as determinative beyond practicality, although doubters questioned whether such insistence on separateness was really justified.

Telshe Yeshiva, reestablished in the Cleveland area after being brutally uprooted from its European home during the war, was never an official communal beneficiary but nevertheless received widespread support from all sections of communal leadership when it faced several crises, including a major fire and an urgent need to relocate its facility. And probably no figure was more venerated by all sectors of the community than Rabbi Israel Porath, dean of the Orthodox Rabbinical Council and honorary Federation trustee, whose serene and witty comments and profound scholarship combined to make him a model both of Jewish distinctiveness and at-homeness in the world of general affairs.

Nevertheless, there were undeniably some continuing feelings of apartness. Only two agencies, Bureau of Jewish Education and JFSA, not under direct Orthodox sponsorship ever had an Orthodox president—for whatever reason. However, Orthodox Jews held other offices, and *yarmulkes* were certainly increasingly evident at meetings of boards and committees everywhere. This was hardly surprising, since skullcaps could for the first time also occasionally be found in academia and in leading institutions of the general community as the Orthodox community increased substantially in affluence and in participation in the life of the general community.

If Orthodox Jews sometimes, though decreasingly, felt they were underrepresented in the larger Jewish community, the Jewish community, though also decreasingly, occasionally felt Orthodoxy was underrepresented when basic responsibilities had to be met, and was sometimes intransigent in insisting on its own point of view.

Orthodoxy benefited from mergers and growing communal cooperation, but the situation in Conservative and Reform congregations was more complex. The boom in synagogue membership faded rapidly in the seventies (a problem also for Orthodox congregations), as the number of children, whose education was a prime motivation for congregational affiliation, declined and economic conditions grew tougher. Total membership in the Conservative congregations fell from 5,000 to 3,600 families in less than a decade, and the decline in Reform membership was comparable. To complicate the picture further, the future promised no relief, since the birthrate continued to decline. It was certain that for at least the next decade no increase in the numbers of children—and, therefore, members—could be expected.

Moreover, there was evidence that the membership of the congregations was growing older. In itself, this was no surprise since all demographic figures revealed that the Jewish community as a whole was older than the general community, but the rate of loss by congregations was disturbing even when that factor was taken into account. The decrease in the numbers of young people in general, and a growing tendency to drop congregational affiliation or to affiliate with new, smaller congregations added to the problems of the older institutions.

Meanwhile, the cost of operating the congregations increased substantially in line with the general and continuing rise in the cost of living, while resistance to higher membership dues also grew, from families

Pinhas Sapir (next to teacher's desk), Israel's minister of finance, took time out during his visit to Cleveland for a speaking engagement to tour the Hebrew Academy, a community Orthodox day school. 1974 (Hebrew Academy)

Presidents and Directors of the Jewish Community Federation, 1977 (Jewish Community Federation)

Top Row: Charles Eisenman, 1903-1923; Edward I. Baker, 1923-1927; Mrs. Siegmund Herzog, 1927-1930; Sol Reinthal, 1930-1933; Louis S. Bing, 1933-1936; Joseph M. Berne, 1936-1945; Henry Rocker, 1945-1953; Max Freedman, 1953-1956.

Second row: Max Simon, 1956-1959; Leo W. Neumark, 1959-1962; Myron E. Glass, 1962-1965; David N. Myers, 1965-1968; Lloyd S. Schwenger, 1968-1971; Maurice Saltzman, 1971-1974; Morton L. Mandel, 1974-1977.

Bottom row: Samuel Goldhamer, 1907-1948; Henry L. Zucker 1948-1965 (Executive Vice President 1965-1975); Sidney Z. Vincent, 1965-1975; Stanley B. Horowitz, 1975-   .

caught in the economic pinch. When it became necessary in 1976 for one of the largest and most firmly established congregations to raise dues, it was estimated that almost half the membership could not be expected to meet the rise in assessments, even though the new figure was not out of line with general increases.

Rising costs and the steep decline in enrollments in their schools constituted major problems for the congregations, particularly since these developments followed a period of substantial growth. Under such circumstances, it was probably inevitable that they should look for some relief to the Federation, which in the seventies was allocating over a million dollars yearly for Jewish education. The 1954 Education Study reported that four out of five students were enrolled in congregational schools, and, since the organized community had declared its interest in Jewish education of all its children, why should not the congregations claim help in their time of trouble? Those so inclined could point to statements like this one, taken from the most recent education study, in 1976:

The majority of Jewish school children (almost three out of four) receive their Jewish education in weekend congregational, not communal schools. The committee throughout its consideration accepted it as a basic principle that the community is interested in *all* its children, who will become the citizens of the future regardless of the school they attend.[25]

At the same time, developments within the Federation seemed to promise an increasingly closer relationship with the interests of the synagogues. Board of Trustees meetings now began with a *D'var Torah* (Biblical homily); all meals served in the building were strictly kosher; leadership development courses explored the Jewish meaning of communal activity; formal courses on Jewish ethics and history, in collaboration with the College of Jewish Studies, were offered at the Federation building. Most important, the vastly increased responsibilities of the Federation, including not only raising many millions of dollars but also involvement in the turbulent affairs of international events, raised basic questions of Jewish commitment. Clearly the line between what were sometimes referred to as "the sacred and the secular" was being obscured. Insofar as synagogue and Federation represented tangible symbols of the sacred and the secular, they were becoming interfused. Congregations were perplexed and worried about their secular (and fiscal) concerns, and the Federation was deeply involved in tasks and responsibilities and objectives that were once thought to be the "turf" of synagogues.

The future posed many problems: Would synagogues be willing or able to give up some degree of their traditional autonomy in return for receiving direct help from the community? Could the community add this fiscal burden without interfering with its responsibility to more traditional agencies and concerns? How in general could these two power centers of Jewish life best cooperate with each other? These were questions that also faced the national community, as could be attested by the establishment of commissions on synagogue-federation relations by both the Council of Jewish Federations and Welfare Funds and the Synagogue Council of America (the Chairman of whose commission was a Clevelander, Rabbi Arthur Lelyveld). It was a good guess that the Cleveland experience would play its usual important role in solving the problem nationally.

Cleveland Jewish News

Since early in the century community developments had been reported in a number of publications, but most notably in three—*The*

Jewish Independent, The Jewish Review and Observer, and the *Yiddishe Velt*. All three were weeklies, although the *Yiddishe Velt* for a period in the twenties published daily.

The two English-language publications were edited and published by two families, the Weidenthals and the Wertheimers. Leo Weidenthal, the editor of *The Independent* for half a century, was throughout his long life more of a nineteenth than a twentieth century man—always formally dressed in black, quiet spoken, a literary scholar and collector of theater artifacts, with an intense distaste for controversy. Howard and Ralph Wertheimer, active for an equally long period at *The Jewish Review and Observer*, had other interests as well, in their printing business and in the world of drama.

In the sixties it became apparent that neither of the papers had kept up with the times, either in circulation or in coverage of the news. A group of community leaders, originally headed by Lloyd S. Schwenger, finally persuaded both families to sell them their publications so that a new, non-profit enterprise could be established that would be better equipped to deal with the fast-breaking events of the community.

The result was the establishment in 1965 of the *Cleveland Jewish News*. Aided by the decision of the Federation to purchase subscriptions for its membership, circulation rose from a few thousand to 16,000, the reporting staff was substantially increased, and the new paper became an important ingredient of the community's life. Arthur Weyne and Jerry Barach served as editors, and Ben D. Zevin and Max M. Axelrod followed Lloyd S. Schwenger as presidents.

A View Toward the Future

The relationship of synagogues and the Federation was obviously only one of many major problems facing the community as it entered the last quarter of a turbulent century. Major shifts in neighborhoods were almost certain to occur. Throughout the century, areas had remained Jewish for only a single generation; more than thirty years had already elapsed since the move "up the hill" began in earnest. The radically changing situation in the western part of the Heights area foreshadowed probable further moves, with all the resultant unsettling effects on a closely knit cluster of institutions and homes. Meanwhile, nationwide population shifts clearly would continue to favor the South and West at the expense of the older midwest communities; numbers would continue to decline, particularly among the younger generation.

The boom times of the postwar period, which had made possible both substantial construction of facilities and a remarkable expansion of services, were over. They had been replaced by a puzzling and disturbing combination of inflation and recession. How long it would be possible to maintain the high standards of communal care and philanthropic giving in the face of restricted incomes was problematical.

Although there was continuing pressure for more precise definition of communal priorities, it was apparent that two broad fields had been singled out for particular care involving unprecedented demands on the community: care of the aged and concern for the Jewish commitment of young people. In the former case, the population would continue to age and techniques would have to be found for completing the cycle of care, from the healthy aged to the incapacitated. In the latter case, Cleveland would join all other communities in the difficult but crucial task of learning how to offset the assimilative temptations of an open society. At the same time, and most important, there would be the complex of challenges facing Jewry everywhere—relationships with Israel, rescuing Soviet Jewry, fighting anti-Semitism, responding to emergencies almost certain to erupt in the coming years, with whole nations and societies in turmoil.

Would Cleveland continue to be, from a Jewish standpoint, one of the best locations in the nation in meeting those challenges? Those who attempted to explain its traditionally preeminent position usually pointed to a number of happy circumstances: its population of 80,000 was small enough to make possible a sense of intimacy and "community," and large enough to permit major undertakings; its extraordinary neighborhood compactness throughout its history, even in suburbia, provided a kind of critical mass deriving from ease of contact and reflected in the warmth of the relationship between laymen and professionals; its leadership displayed astonishing stability.

This last point may be the most significant. The pulpit of The Temple had been occupied by the Rabbis Silver (Abba Hillel followed by Daniel J.) since 1917 and seemed likely to continue that way indefinitely; of the other three giant congregations, Rabbi Armond E. Cohen had headed Park Synagogue and Rabbi Rudolph M. Rosenthal the Temple on the Heights since 1934. Both grew up in Cleveland and neither had ever held any other pulpit. Rabbi Barnett R. Brickner was senior rabbi of Fairmount Temple from 1925 until his death in 1958, when he was succeeded by Rabbi Arthur J. Lelyveld. Rabbi Alan Green, another native Clevelander, had served Temple Emanu El since its founding in 1946; Rabbi Myron Silverman of Suburban Temple (with the exception of a single year) and Rabbi Philip Horowitz of B'rith Emeth were also the only men ever to head their congregations. In the Orthodox community, Rabbis Louis Engelberg, Shubert Spero, and Jacob Muskin had

all served more than a quarter-century, and Rabbis Israel Porath and David L. Genuth headed their congregations for still longer periods, until their deaths.

A similar condition of communal longevity obtained in the agencies. When Henry L. Zucker and Sidney Z. Vincent retired in 1975, it was pointed out that the Federation had been under only two professional administrations since its founding in 1903, and with the appointment of Stanley B. Horowitz to succeed them there was the possibility that the entire century might pass with only three administrations. (All three men, as well as Samuel Goldhamer, the first executive director, were native Clevelanders—a record unparalleled anywhere.) The record for long service by the professional heads of the other agencies was less dramatic, but certainly tended in the same direction. Executives came to the Cleveland community to stay—most of them for the rest of their professional lives.

In the long run, the staying power of the laymen was probably the decisive factor in the preeminence of Cleveland's Jewish community. Men and women rose to the top of their organizations, served as presidents, and then did not retire to the sidelines but continued to be highly active. Again, the Federation presidency can be viewed as typical. In the thirty years covered in this essay, nine men served as presidents, eight of them either native Clevelanders or brought to the city as children from overseas. Of the seven still living in 1976, all remained devoted and active in communal affairs. It was a prized tradition in the community's life.

No one illustrated that lifelong dedication better than the layman whose personality clearly dominated the period. It seems appropriate to conclude this narrative with the tribute paid to him on his death in 1975:[26]

1.

2.

1. Cantor Saul Meisels' family emigrated from Poland to the United States in 1918. Educated in New York, he came to Cleveland to Congregation B'nai Jeshurun in 1942. He enriched Jewish musical life, representing a distinguished Cleveland tradition in Jewish liturgy developed together with his colleagues over many decades. ca. 1972 (Saul Meisels)

2. A family tradition of service is represented in this photograph of Leonard Ratner, outstanding community leader for a generation, with his son, Albert, then general chairman of the Jewish Welfare Fund and elected five years later president of the Federation. 1972 (Jewish Community Federation)

Leonard Ratner was the acknowledged leader of our community, both as man and as symbol.

As symbol, he bridged the gap between two eras of Jewish life. Born into an old-world environment, he drew from it life-long nourishment . . . powerful traditions of family integrity and warmth, social responsibility, service to mankind and total loyalty to his religious heritage.

Translated to modern, bustling America, his adaptation to his new life was complete, without any lessening of the conviction he brought with him. He made his way in Cleveland in business, in the general community, in the synagogue . . . combining the best of the old with the best of the new. He was the classic example of the American experience through which talented immigrants become creative Americans, creative Jews and creative human beings.

But it is Leonard Ratner the man whom we loved . . . Leonard chatting with Golda Meir and with working people, equally at home with both . . . the singer of Sabbath melodies, the kindly, teasing friend of all children, his hands full of magnificent gifts for every type of charitable effort as well as pieces of candy for all.

He was in every sense the complete father of his family . . . both his personal family, to whom he was utterly devoted, and the extended family of his own community . . . of Jews everywhere and of all men.

He was a blessing to us all his life . . . he will remain a blessing to us forever.

There would never be another leader precisely like Leonard Ratner, since the world that produced him had been shattered. Nevertheless, the long-lasting and sturdy traditions of the community he had served so well constituted the best promise that Cleveland would continue to play a vital role in the life of the American Jewish community.

1.   Eugene J. Lipman and Albert Vorspan, eds.,
*A Tale of Ten Cities, the Triple Ghetto in American Religious
Life* (New York, 1962), pp. 45–77.

2.   The predictions that Cleveland would drop to
seventeenth in size by 1980 proved an understatement.
The governmental mid-decennial census reported
that it had already fallen to that spot by 1975 and would
undoubtedly drop lower since its loss in population was
second greatest in percentage of the fifty largest cities in
the nation. (United States Bureau of Census in the
Cleveland *Plain Dealer*, Cleveland, Ohio, April 14, 1977).

3.   In 1969–1970, the following Clevelanders served
as presidents of national organizations: Jordan C. Band
(National Jewish Community Relations Advisory Coun-
cil); Isabel Brown (International Council of Jewish
Women); Edward Ginsberg (United Jewish Appeal);
Irving Kane (American Israel Public Affairs Committee);
Rabbi Arthur J. Lelyveld (American Jewish Congress);
Morton L. Mandel (National Jewish Welfare Board);
Rabbi Daniel J. Silver (National Foundation for Jewish
Culture); Sidney Z. Vincent (National Conference of
Jewish Communal Service).

4.   The professional directors of the Federations of
the largest communities on the continent established an
informal organization known as "The Big Sixteen." Of
the fourteen in the United States (excluding Montreal
and Toronto) during the period under review, seven
were native Clevelanders or grew up in Cleveland: James
Rice of Chicago, Henry L. Zucker of Cleveland, William
Avrunin of Detroit, Ben Rosenberg of Boston, Donald
Hurwitz of Philadelphia, David Rabinowitz of St. Louis,
and Arthur Rosichan of Miami. Three became executives
of other communities directly after serving in a major
capacity in the Cleveland Federation: Robert I. Hiller of
Baltimore, Gerald Soroker of Pittsburgh, and Bernard
Olshansky, who succeeded Rosenberg in Boston. (Irwin
Gold of Toronto also fits in this category.) And three
served in other Cleveland organizations before becoming
directors of Federations elsewhere: Sanford Solender of
New York earlier headed the Jewish Community Center;
Alvin Bronstein of Los Angeles served as field director of
the Council of Jewish Federations and Welfare Funds;
and Abe Sudran of Newark directed the Jewish Vocational
Service. Only San Francisco and Washington had no
"Cleveland connection."

In addition, two major national organizations were
headed professionally by former associate directors of
the Federation: Philip Bernstein of the Council of Jewish
Federations and Welfare Funds and John Slawson of
the American Jewish Committee.

5.   Perhaps the most striking example of the wide
influence of Rabbi Goldman on the intellectual life of
the community was his formation of the Dayot (knowledge) Club, bringing together for monthly meetings
some forty members from all sections of the community
for discussion of philosophical issues.

6.   For a detailed description of life in "the old days"
in the Kinsman area, see "How Life Was Among 'the
Kinsman Cowboys,' " by Harold Ticktin, *The Cleveland
Jewish News*, January 7, 1972, and "More Memories of
'the Kinsman Cowboys,' " by Violet Spevack, *ibid.*,
January 21, 1972.

7.   The three Glenville councilmen were Harry
Marshall (24th Ward), Harry Jaffe (25th Ward), and Victor Cohen (27th Ward).

8.   Joseph H. Silbert and Alvin I. Krenzler served
on the Court of Appeals; Adrian B. Fink, Jr., Bernard
Friedman, Harry Jaffe, and Harry T. Marshall served on
the Court of Common Pleas.

9.   Among the many examples of non-elective but
significant political activity during this period were
Howard M. Metzembaum, campaign manager for United
States Senator Stephen M. Young; Leo Ascherman, who
served in the same capacity for William McDermott in his
unsuccessful campaign for Mayor of Cleveland; Samuel
H. Miller, Rabbi Daniel J. Silver, Max Axelrod, and
David Skylar, all of whom served as chairmen of the
Cuyahoga County Grand Jury.

10.   See Eli E. Cohen, "Economic Status and Occupational Structure," *American Jewish Yearbook*, vol. 51 (1950),
pp. 53–70; Council of Jewish Federations and Welfare
Funds, National Jewish Population Study, "Demo-
graphic Highlights, Facts for Planning" (c. 1975); Jewish
Community Federation of Cleveland, "Table 6. Occupa-
tional Distribution of Cleveland Jewish Population,"
Population Report 1970. For additional data and inter-
pretation of Jewish economic mobility before 1960, see
Section 2, "Demographic Aspects and the Factor of
Social Mobility," in *The Jews, Social Patterns of an American
Group*, ed. Marshall Sklare (Glencoe, Illinois, 1958).

11. For the complete testimony on housing discrimination against Jews, see Jewish Community Federation of Cleveland, Minutes of the Board of Trustees, June 6, 1962.

12. Extensive description and analysis of the United Freedom Movement, and the relation of the Jewish community to it, are contained in the Jewish Community Federation of Cleveland, Minutes of the Board of Trustees, September 25, 1963; April 29, 1964; February 1, 1967. The quotation by Bennett Yanowitz, the chairman of the Community Relations Committee at that time, appears in the latter set of Minutes, p. 111.

13. Lipman and Vorspan, *Tale of Ten Cities*, p. 75.

14. Henry L. Zucker, "A Ten Year Look at the Jewish Community Federation of Cleveland, 1946–1956."

15. Bureau of Jewish Education, Cleveland, Ohio, Minutes of the Board of Trustees, November 7, 1938.

16. Eric Rosenthal, "Studies of Jewish Intermarriage in the United States," *American Jewish Yearbook*, vol. 64 (1963), pp. 3–53; Arnold Schwartz, "Intermarriage in the United States," *American Jewish Yearbook*, vol. 71 (1970), pp. 101–121; Council of Jewish Federations and Welfare Funds, National Jewish Population Study, "Intermarriage Facts for Planning" (c. 1975).

17. Social agencies in 1975 supported by the Jewish Welfare Fund included nine educational agencies—Agnon School, Akiva High School, Bureau of Jewish Education, College of Jewish Studies, Cleveland Hebrew Schools, Hebrew Academy, United Jewish Religious Schools, Workmen's Circle School (Yiddish oriented), and Yeshivath Adath B'nai Israel (afternoon Hebrew school); three centers for care of the aged—Jewish Convalescent and Rehabilitation Center, Menorah Park and Montefiore Home; four youth-serving agencies—Bellefaire, B'nai B'rith Hillel Foundation, B'nai B'rith Youth Organization, and Jewish Children's Bureau; Jewish Community Center; Jewish Family Service Association; Jewish Vocational Service; Mt. Sinai Hospital; and the Hebrew Shelter Home. In addition the Hebrew Free Loan Association and Council Gardens were communal agencies with representation on Federation committees, although they were not direct beneficiaries.

18. Statement of Sanford Solender, Executive Director of the Council Educational Alliance, in Minutes of the Executive Committee, June 21, 1943.

19. *Ibid.*

20. Kinoy's statement is contained in Council Educational Alliance, Minutes of the Camp Wise Executive Committee, July 14, 1936; Gold's, in Jewish Community Center, Minutes of the Camp Wise Committee, August 25, 1949.

21. Camp Wise, Minutes of the Board of Trustees, June 28, 1945.

22. *Ibid.*

23. Urban League quote.

24. Albert B. Ratner, Letter of Transmittal (February 26, 1976), in Report of the Jewish Education Study Committee of the Jewish Community Federation of Cleveland, p. 11.

25. *Ibid.*

26. *The Cleveland Jewish News*, January 3, 1975.

II

A Pictorial Record
1839–1975

The Beginnings

God will send His angel before thee,
There shall no evil befall thee.
In all thy ways acknowledge Him,
And He will direct thy paths . . . .

I further wish and hope that the Almighty,
who reigns over the ocean as well as over dry
land, to whom thunder and storms must pay
heed, shall give you good angels as travel
companions, so that you, my dear friends,
may arrive undisturbed and healthy in body
and soul at the place of your destiny, in
the land of freedom.

But I must also, as a friend, ask a favor of
you.

Friends! You are traveling to a land of freedom where the opportunity will be presented
to live without compulsory religious education.

Resist and withstand this tempting freedom
and do not turn away from the religion of
our fathers. Do not throw away your holy
religion for quickly lost earthly pleasures,
because your religion brings you consolation
and quiet in this life and it will bring you
happiness for certain in the other life . . . .

Your friend,
Lazarus Kohn, Teacher

Unsleben near Neustadt on the Saale in
Lower Franconia in the Kingdom of Bavaria
the 5th of May 1839.

From the Ethical Testament addressed to
Moses and Jetta Alsbacher and the
Unsleben Company of Immigrants

1.

2.

The Cleveland Jewish community was founded by immigrants from the town of Unsleben, Bavaria, who left during the high period of German-Jewish migration. Addressed to Moses (1) and Jetta Alsbacher, the ethical testament (2) exhorts the emigrants to remember those left behind and to guard against loss of their faith in a land of tempting freedom (1-*Jewish Independent*; 2-Jewish Community Federation)

1.

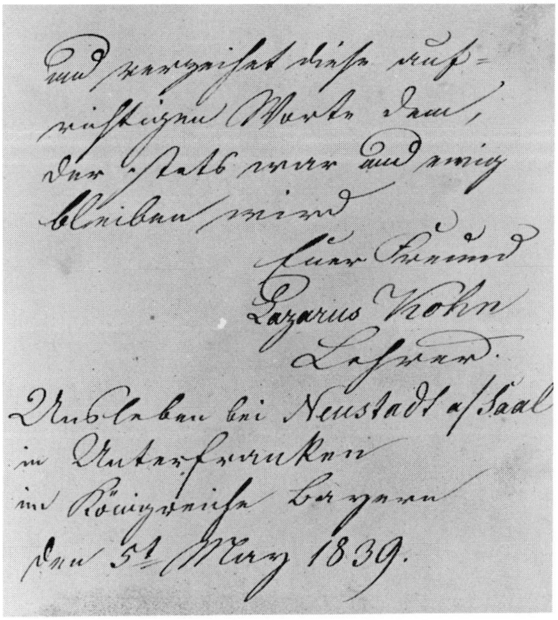

und verzeihet diese auf=
richtigen Worte dem,
der stets war und ewig
bleiben wird
Euer Freund
Lazarus Kohn
Lehrer.
Unsleben bei Neustadt a/Saal
in Unterfranken
im Königreiche Bayern
den 5t May 1839.

2.

3.

45.

Die Gesellschaft der Aus=
wanderer:

1. Moses Alsbacher
2. Jetta Frau
3. Zittle Tochter
4. Simson Hoffmann
5. Sara, Frau
6. [illegible], [illegible]
7. Vögele } Töchter
8. Zerle
9. Mayer } Thormanns
10. Simmle } Kinder
11. Reule

13. Simson Thorman ist schon in Amerika

1. The testament is signed by Lazarus Kohn, teacher of the Unsleben community, and is dated 5 May, 1839. (Jewish Community Federation)

2. The document lists the 18 members of the company of emigrants, most of whom came to Cleveland, and notes that Simson Thorman is already in America. (Jewish Community Federation)

3. Simson Thorman (1812–1881), who traded in furs as far west as Missouri, made Cleveland his home base in 1837 and undoubtedly influenced the Unsleben immigrants to settle here. n.d. (*Jewish Independent*)

Simson Thorman married Regina Klein (d. 1885), one of the Unsleben group, soon after she arrived in Cleveland. Their son Samuel, the first of their twelve children, was the first Jewish child born in the city. The photographs of Simson and Regina are tintypes encased in a locket. ca. 1855 (Mrs. Ethel Kendis)

The Unsleben company departed Hamburg in June, 1839, on the ship *Howard* and arrived in New York, July 12th. The ship's manifest of passengers lists the members of the Unsleben group by age and vocation along with a description of their baggage. (Western Reserve Historical Society)

NOTICE.—Messrs. Perez B. Wolcott and William D. Colburn having by mutual consent withdrawn from the firm of Wolcott, Colburn & Co., the said copartnership was this day dissolved. The business of the concern will be settled by Lewis Joachimssen, who, jointly with Mr. Philip J. Joachimssen will carry on the wholesale Grocery and Liquor Business at the old stand of Messrs. Wolcott, Colburn & Co., under the firm of

Oct 12 [oct17]   JOACHIMSSEN & CO.

JOACHIMSSEN & CO. have just received their stock of New Goods, and offer for sale to the trade, at reasonable prices, on a credit of two and four monts, a general assortment of FISH, COFFEE, SUGARS, WINES, LIQUORS, HERRINGS, RAISINS, TOBACCO, SEGARS, &c. which they recommend as superior articles.   [oct 17

LIQUORS, WINES, &c.—Just received and for sale low for cash or approved credit, a large assortment of Liquors, Wines, &c., among which are the following, viz:

St. Croix Rum,	Cognac Brandy,
Jamaica do.	Holland Gin,
Cherry do.	

WINES.

Champaigne,	Old Port,
Old Madeira,	Common do.
Common do.	Raspberry,
Sicily do.	Malaga,
Raisins,	Tobacco, Cigars.

Domestic Liquors constantly on hand,
All of which are warranted a superior article and for sale by JOACHIMSSEN & CO.

Oct 17

ALSO

For sale as above, on consignment, 8 day brass time pieces, 30 hour Clocks, do., 8 day wood, do., all warranted and will be sold low for cash.

N. B. One of the partners, (Louis Joachimssen, Esq.,) residing in New York, will select and purchase Goods for the firm, which will enable them, at all times, to furnish articles in their line, of the best quality and at the lowest prices.

FISH.—JOACHIMSSEN & CO., Store on the wharf, three doors below Ward & Smith, offer for sale on reasonable terms,

50 bbls. of Mackerel, in whole, half and quarte; bbls, Nos. 1 2, and 3;

12 bbls. new pickled Salmon;

300 lbs. dried Codfish;

100 boxes Herrings;

50 do. Shad;

10 bbls. Maine Shad, in whole and half bbls.

Oct 17

JOACHIMSSEN & CO. have just received and offer for sale to the trade for cash and on approved credit of two and four months, a general assortment of DRY GROCERIES, Li-

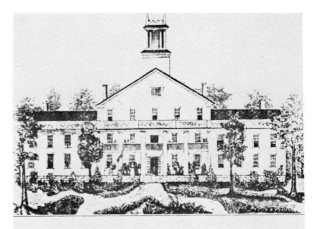

THE WILLOUGHBY UNIVERSITY

BUILT IN 1836

The central section shown in this architect's sketch was occupied by Willoughby Medical School from 1836 to 1847 and by Willoughby Female Seminary from 1847 to 1856. The wings and the portico on the central portion were additions proposed in 1851, but were never actually built. The building burned on March 4, 1856.

1. Earliest evidence of Jews in Cleveland is found in an advertisement in the Cleveland *Herald*, October 18, 1836, by Philip and Lewis Joachimssen, grocery and liquor merchants. Originally from Breslau, Germany, they departed Cleveland after their business failed in the Panic of 1837. Philip, at least, resumed his career successfully in New York City. (Cleveland *Herald*)

2. Dr. Daniel Levy Maduro Peixotto (1800–1842) of Spanish-Jewish descent; was a member of the Willoughby Medical School faculty from 1836 to about 1841. n.d. (Western Reserve Historical Society)

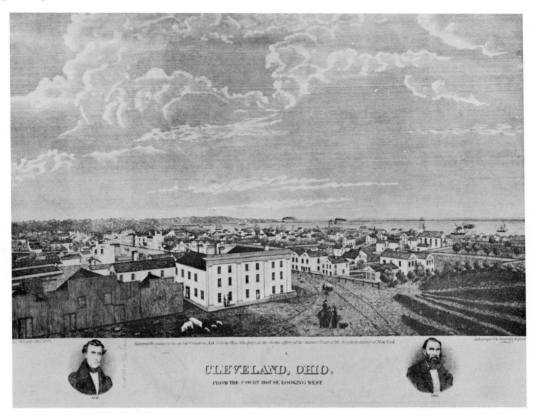

CLEVELAND, OHIO,
FROM THE COURT HOUSE LOOKING WEST

This view of Cleveland, etched by Thomas Whelpley in 1833, was essentially the one which the Unsleben immigrants saw when they reached the city, most likely by way of the Erie Canal and lake steamer. (Western Reserve Historical Society)

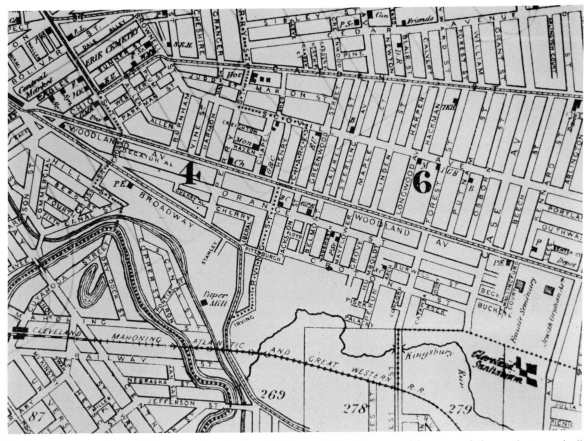

The first immigrants clustered in homes in the vicinity of the Central Market. As more of them arrived, the population gradually moved eastward along streets radiating from this center of earliest settlement—Orange, Woodland, Scovill and Garden (Central). 1869 (Cleveland Directory)

1.

2.

3.

AN ACT

To incorporate the Anshi Chesmed Congregation of the city of Cleveland.

SEC. 1. *Be it enacted by the General Assembly of the State of Ohio,* That Asher Lehman, Simon Seaman, Jacob L. Richard, Michael Winner, Moses Manasses, Samuel Dettinhoeffer, Ephraim Dettinhoeffer, and Gelson Strouse, and their associates and successors, and those who may hereafter be associated with them, be and they are hereby created a body politic and corporate, by the name of the Anshi Chesmed Congregation of the city of Cleveland; and, as such, shall be entitled to all the rights, privileges, and immunities granted by, and be subject to all the restrictions contained in, act entitled "an act in relation to incorporated religious societies," passed March fifth, one thousand eight hundred and thirty six.

SEC. 2. That ten days previous notice of the time and place of holding their first meeting under this act shall be given, by posting up advertisements, signed by a majority of the above named corporators, in at least five public places in said city of Cleveland.

RUFUS P. SPALDING,
Speaker of the House of Representatives.
JAMES J. FARAN,
Speaker of the Senate.

February 28, 1842.

1. After organizing as a religious community, the Israelitic Society purchased land for a burial ground in Ohio City from Josiah Barber. The Willet Street Cemetery is located at W. 22nd Street and Fulton Road. 1975 (Richard E. Karberg)

2. The first Jewish landmark in Cleveland was naturally a synagogue. As soon as membership and resources permitted, the reunited Israelitic Anshe Chesed Society employed John Wigman, master builder, to construct the congregation's own home. The Eagle Street synagogue, a modified version of the local Baptist church, was erected on the south side of Eagle Street and dedicated August 7-8, 1846. Its dimensions: 35 feet front, 32 feet high, 50 feet deep. n.d. (*Jewish Review and Observer*)

3. A group from the original Society seceded in 1841, most likely in disagreement over religious practices, and was chartered as the Anshe Chesed Society in 1842. It rejoined the parent body in 1845 after a fire destroyed its place of worship. (Western Reserve Historical Society)

1.

2.

3.

Wegweiſer

für

rationelle Forſchungen

in den

biblischen Schriften,

oder

was lehrt das Urchriſtenthum, und was
der Moſaismus?

Von

Iſidor Kaliſch,

Rabbiner und Prediger.

Motto: Weisheit iſt freie Prüfung des Gewöhnlichen.
Peter Charron.

Selig der Mann, der weiſe nachdenkt, und nach
der Vernunft ſich führt.
Sirach 14, 22.

Selbſtverlag des Verfaſſers.

1. The pattern of Reform Judaism in Cleveland took shape in the 19th Century with the formation in 1850 of Congregation Tifereth Israel by a splinter group from the Anshe Chesed-Eagle Street Congregation. Their Huron Street Synagogue on the corner of Miami (E. 6th) and Huron was dedicated in 1856. (Jewish Community Federation)

2. Rabbi Isidor Kalisch (1816–1886), Cleveland's first rabbi who served at both the Eagle Street and Huron Street congregations, was also its first Jewish author. (American Jewish Archives, Cincinnati)

3. Kalisch's *Wegweiser für rationelle Forschungen in den Biblischen Schriften* was published in Cleveland in 1853. It was translated into English as *A Guide for Rational Inquiries into the Biblical Writings* in 1857. (American Jewish Archives, Cincinnati)

1.

2.

3.

1.   Gustavus M. Cohen (1820–1902), trained in music and pedagogy in Germany, was a *chazzan* (cantor) first at the Eagle Street Synagogue and then at the Huron Street congregation. Organizer of the Zion Musical Society and a composer of religious music, Cohen published *The Sacred Harp of Judah* in 1864, the second book by a Cleveland Jewish resident. (American Jewish Archives, Cincinnati)

2.   One of the earliest Orthodox congregations, Anshe Emeth, was established by Jews from Poland in 1868. In 1883, the congregation advertised in the national *Jewish Messenger* for a " 'chazzan,' reader and teacher competent to teach a Sabbath school and lecture in English or German (both preferred)." Rabbi David Levy was apparently engaged by the congregation to fill this multiple position at a starting salary of "$1,000 per annum, and perquisites." ca. 1905 (Florence and Annette Benjamin)

3.   The earliest known Jewish wedding photograph is that of Esther Thorman (1842–1907) and Edward Budwig dating from the early 1860s. Esther and her sister, Lizzie (Mrs. Kaufman Hays), were the first Jewish twins born in Cleveland.

Edward Budwig was a partner with his father-in-law, Simson Thorman, in the latter's commission business. Later in the decade, he went alone to California and Mexico for health reasons and engaged in various mining enterprises. This prolonged separation from Esther led to their subsequent divorce. ca. 1862 (Mrs. Ethel Kendis)

1.

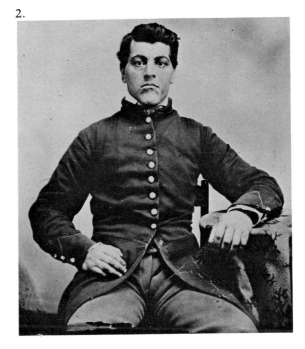

3.

2.

1. The first Cleveland Jew documented in military service was Jacob Arnstein (1819–1879) from Bavaria and a peddler by trade. During the Mexican war, he enlisted in Captain Irvine's Company, Ohio 4th Regiment at Millersburg, Ohio. After discharge in July, 1848, he came to Cleveland, where he received a 160-acre land grant. (Abe L. Nebel Collection, Western Reserve Historical Society)

2. During the Civil War, 38 Cleveland Jews served in the Union forces; others settled in the city after the war, including Morris Ullman and Felix Rosenberg, who fought for the Confederacy.

Jacob Brown (1835–1904), shown here, first enlisted in the 55th Regiment, Ohio Volunteer Infantry, at Norwalk in 1861. He was captured at Chancellorsville, May, 1863, and was paroled the same month. After reenlistment he was wounded at Resaca, Virginia, in May, 1864, and received his disability discharge in Cleveland. ca. 1864 (Mrs. Charles Cohen)

3. Aaron Marx (1834–1901) enlisted at Erie, Pennsylvania. He settled in Cleveland after the war and was the city's first Jewish policeman. (Abe L. Nebel Collection, Western Reserve Historical Society)

1.

2.

1.   Edward Rosewater (1841–1906), a member of the Cleveland Rosenwasser family, was a clerk in Loeb Colman's clothing store. He learned telegraphy here, became a railroad telegrapher, and served in the War Department Communication Center during the Civil War. He transmitted President Lincoln's Emancipation Proclamation in 1863, which is staged in this photographic reenactment. After the war, he settled in Omaha and later founded the newspaper, the *Omaha Daily Bee*. n.d. (American Jewish Archives, Cincinnati)

2.   Sigmund Shlesinger (1848–1928) emigrated from Hungary to the United States with his parents in 1864. He drifted to Kansas and was a sutler in the camp of the 10th U.S. Cavalry. Out of funds, he joined Col. George Forsythe's company of frontier scouts in 1868 and participated in the Battle of Beecher Island in Colorado, defeating the Cheyenne Chief Roman Nose. "The young son of Israel" was cited for bravery and described as "a worthy descendant of King David." ca. 1875 (American Jewish Archives, Cincinnati)

FRIDAY, SEPTEMBER 18, 1868.

in the night I dug my hole
dipper cut of meat oof of
the Horses hung it up on
Bushes, Indians made a Charge
on us at Day break, but
retreated kept shooting near-
ly all day they Put up a
White Flag, left us
at 9 o clock in Evening
Raind all night

SATURDAY 19

the Indians came
back aguin Kept
sharp shooting all
day 2 Boys started
for Fort Wallace
Raind all night

SUNDAY 20

Dr Moore died last
night Raining
Part of the Day
snow about 2
inches thick
Indians Kept sharp
shooting

MONDAY, SEPTEMBER 21, 1868.

scalped 3 Indians
which where found
about 15 Feet from
my hole conceald
in Grass

TUESDAY 22

Killd a Coyote & eat
him all up

WEDNESDAY 23

In his diary of the battle, Shlesinger recounts scalping three Indians and killing and eating a coyote. He left the army the same year and came to Cleveland in 1870, where he achieved a notable career in business and as a Jewish communal leader. (American Jewish Archives, Cincinnati)

1.

CLEVELAND CHERRY VALLEY
OIL COMPANY.

Capital - - - $500,000.

50,000 Shares. Par Value $10.
SUBSCRIPTION PRICE, $5 —NO FURTHER AS-
SESSMENTS.

WORKING CAPITAL.........$20,000.

B. F. PEIXOTTO, President,
EDWARD BUDWIG, Secretary.
C. KOCH, Treasurer.
TRUSTEES.
B. F. PEIXOTTO, of Davis, Peixotto & Co.
C. KOCH, of Koch, Levi & Mayer.
R. C. YATES, of Tod, Yates & Co.
MANUEL HALLE, of M. Halle & Co.
N. PAYNE, of Cross, Payne & Co.
S. MANN, of S. Mann.
EDWARD BUDWIG, of S. Thorman & Co.
DESCRIPTION OF PROPERTY.
The Lands and Oil Wells connected therewith are
located in Venango County, Penn
Fifty-six acres (in fee simple) lie within a short
walk of Oil Creek, above Oil City, west of the cel-
ebrated Clapp, Buchanan, Rynd, McClintock and
Story farms on which are located the largest produc-
ing and flowing wells in the country. Wells are
now being sunk on this and.
Two other tracts lie immediately on the Alleghany
River, one mile above Oil City on the Altora Farm.
The Company have a lease running ninety-nine
years.
Two new Wells have been sunk on these tracts.

2.

3.

SECOND
SUCCOTH FESTIVAL!
BY THE
Y. M. H. L. SOCIETY!
At their Hall, 184 Superior Street,
TUESDAY EVENING, SEPT. 24th, 1861.

GRAND OVERTURE, - - - - - BILLSON'S BAND.

FAVORITE SONG, - - - - - MISS CAROLINE WOLF.

Sir Edward Lytton Bulwer's beautiful Play in 5 acts, entitled

THE LADY OF LYONS!
OR,
LOVE AND PRIDE.

CLAUDE MELNOTTE	MR B. F. PEIXOTTO.
Beauseant	Mr S A. Tuch
Glavis	Mr. A. Straus
Col. Damas	Mr. A. Moses
Mons. Deschapelles	Mr. A. Wiener
Gaspar	Mr J. W. Riglander
Captain Gervais, 1st officer	Mr. S. Schloss
Captain Dupont, 2d do.	Mr J. Shrier
Major Desmoulins, 3d do.	Mr. S. Thorman
Landlord	Mr. K. Hays
PAULINE	**MISS C. WOLF**
Madame Deschapelles	Miss E Thorman
Widow Melnotte	Miss Fanny Wolf

1. Joining together as entrepreneurs during the Pennsylvania oil boom of the 1860s, several prominent Cleveland Jews organized the Cherry Valley Oil Company with Benjamin F. Peixotto as president. As the notice indicates, the company was capitalized at $500,000. (Cleveland *Plain Dealer*, January 5, 1865)

2. Benjamin Franklin Peixotto (1834–1890), son of Dr. David L. M. Peixotto, was a journalist for the *Plain Dealer*, a successful businessman, and an even more prominent communal leader, until he moved to New York in 1867. He was appointed consul to Bucharest, Rumania, in 1870 by President Grant. n.d. (American Jewish Archives. Cincinnati)

3. Peixotto had a special interest in cultural activities, organizing the Young Men's Hebrew Literary Society in 1860. According to the Society's playbill for Succoth, 1861, its literary focus was English and Peixotto one of its leading actors. (Jewish Community Federation)

1. Many early Cleveland Jews began their careers as peddlers of Yankee notions. Those who succeeded often became proprietors of small stores—groceries, dry-goods, clothing. Others began as clerks or got their start elsewhere and came to city to establish businesses of their own.

Loeb Colman (Kallman) opened his store at 30 Prospect Street in 1847, seven years after arriving from Bavaria. His sign reflects the immigrant neighborhood in which he located. ca. 1880 (Charles Colman)

2. Some settlers gained prominence in other areas of the business world. Among the early settlers, Simson Thorman and his partners, Kaufman Hays and Edward Budwig, by the time of the Civil War, were operating a prosperous business in the near West Side area as commission merchants and dealers in hides and furs. The 1860 census listed Thorman's worth at $10,000 in personal estate and $10,000 in real estate. 1863 (Boyd's Cleveland Directory)

3. The Civil War revived a sagging Cleveland clothing industry. Here Moses Nusbaum and two competitors in the West 3rd-Superior area display army clothing. The second floor of the building served as Cleveland City Hall from 1855–74. (M. Joplin, Cleveland Past and Present)

1.

2.

1.   Morris Ullman emigrated from Wurtenburg at age 16 and was admitted to citizenship in Guilford County, North Carolina, in 1857. After the war he moved north to Youngstown and then to Cleveland, where in 1869 he and his brother, Emanuel, established a wholesale liquor business. Relatives Leopold and Herman Einstein, in the same business, merged with the Ullmans and established the firm which existed until prohibition. The Ullman-Einstein building in this line drawing was located at 69–71 Michigan Street (Terminal Tower area). ca. 1882 (Rufus M. Ullman)

2.   In addition to being liquor distributors, Ullman-Einstein manufactured liquor under their own Black Cat label. The recipe book of their master distiller contains one for Ohio grape brandy. (Rufus M. Ullman)

FANCY GOODS AND TOY BAZAAR.

GRAND OPENING

OF

LEVY & STEARNS'

FANCY GOODS

AND

TOY BAZAAR,

162, 166 and 168 Superior street,

COMMENCING **THURSDAY,** October 16,

And continuing until Saturday Evening.

We shall deem it a great pleasure to welcome our patrons and the public generally to our New Holiday Quarters.

P. S.—In securing the large double store lately vacated by Adams & Goodwille, and which will be devoted solely to the display of our Holiday Fancy Goods and Toy Departments, we are enabled to do justice to our immense assortment of these goods, and offer such a display in this line as has never before been witnessed in Cleveland.

CLOTHING.	AMUSEMENTS

1. Sigmund Mann opened a clothing store on West Superior in the mid-1850s. By the end of the decade he began to manufacture ready-made clothing and expanded his operations to employ approximately 200 employees. Mann in 1885 was included in a *Plain Dealer* list of local millionaires. ca. 1880 (The Temple Archives)

2. The firm of Isaac Levy and Abraham Stearn, importers and dealers in fancy goods, toys, wooden and willow ware, trace their origins back to 1867 to the firm of Moses, Levy & Co. It became Levy and Stearn in 1872, and later Stearn & Co. located on Euclid Avenue. 1879 (Cleveland *Plain Dealer*)

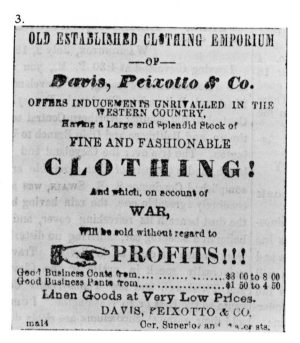

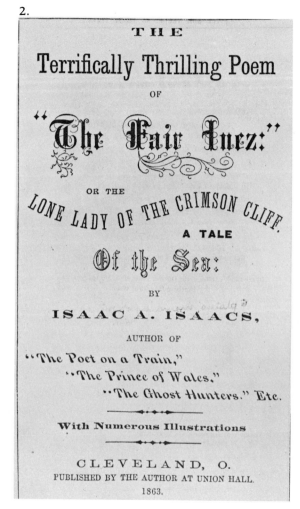

1. The enthusiasm for a new country is reflected in names of stores chosen by Jewish owners. Joel Engelhart's American Eagle Clothing Store at 172 Superior typifies this mood, as did firm names such as Sonneborn's Young America Clothing House, George A. Davis' Oak Hall, Isaac A. Isaacs' Union Hall and Sigmund Mann's Great Western Clothing Hall. West Superior past the Public Square was the center of the clothing trade. 1859 (Cleveland *Plain Dealer*)

2. Isaac A. Isaacs was perhaps Cleveland's most unusual merchant clothier in the 19th century. Born in Boston in 1825, he came to Cleveland in the 1840s and quickly earned a reputation for advertising in verse during the Civil War years. The *Plain Dealer* called him "the most prolific poet in the West." "The Fair Inez," published in 1863, is a verse epic describing a clothing salesman's travels, intermixing business, moral, and patriotic sentiments. In 1865 Isaacs closed out his business and returned east to New York City. (Western Reserve Historical Society)

3. George A. Davis, born in England, reached Cleveland by 1850. He expanded his retail clothing manufacturing business in 1857, when Raphael Peixotto became his partner. Davis, Peixotto & Co. closed shop about 1866, with first Davis and then Peixotto moving to New York City. 1861 (City Directory)

ISAAC A. ISAACS.

IMPORTER & JOBBER OF CLOTHS, CASSIMERES,

VESTINGS AND TAILORS' TRIMMINGS.

MANUFACTURER & DEALER IN READY MADE CLOTHING

AND FURNISHING GOODS,

UNION HALL,
Corner Superior and Union Sts., CLEVELAND, O.

This line drawing of Union Hall at Superior and West 10th, then Union Lane, suggests the scope of Isaacs' enterprise as a clothing merchant and manufacturer and franchise agent for the Singer Sewing Machine and a patented army trunk and bed. 1861 (City Directory)

1.

2.

1.   Kaufman Hays (1835–1916) reached Cleveland in 1852 to join his sister, Rosa, who preceded him. He started out as a clerk in a clothing store but turned to peddling as a quicker means of accumulating capital. After building a successful clothing business, which he sold, Hays turned to banking and was an organizer of the First National Bank of Cleveland and the Cleveland Worsted Mills. He was a prominent civic leader, serving for a period as city treasurer and vice-president of City Council. ca. 1885 (Nancy Jacobs)

2.   Elias Cohen (1824–1904) was the first Cleveland Jew to make a business career in lake shipping, starting in 1860 with the acquisition of a passenger vessel, the *Lady Franklin*, and later several lake freighters. He started out in the clothing business shortly after settling in Cleveland in 1846. (*Jewish Review and Observer*, May 27, 1904)

Many German immigrants were skilled in cigar making. A news report of a Cigar Makers Union strike in 1880 lists 27 firms including that of Jacob and Bernhard Rohrheimer from Hesse Darmstadt, who were identified in the 1863–64 city directory as "segarmakers." They established their own manufactory in 1865 at 101 Superior, where this photograph was taken. ca. 1880 (Frank E. Joseph)

1.

sep3:6w W

NOTICE

OUR STORE WILL BE CLOSED

THURSDAY, SEPTEMBER 18th,

ON ACCOUNT OF HOLIDAYS.

M. Halle & Co.,

147 WATER STREET.

LIQUOR DEALER.

3.

SITUATION WANTED—A Jewish boy 15 years old who speaks and writes English and German and resides with his mother, would like a permanent situation where he can learn a good trade. Address A. A., PLAIN DEALER office. my11?

WANTED—SITUATION—As general housemaid or second helper; aged 19. Apply at 25 King street, Cleveland, O.   m9f

2.

1. Notices and want ads in the local newspapers occasionally reflected the Jewish presence in Cleveland. Moses Halle & Co. announced its closing for an unspecified holiday in the *Plain Dealer* of September 17, 1879. The Jewish New Year, 1 Tishri 5640, began the prior evening. (Cleveland *Plain Dealer*)

2. By the turn of the century Cleveland was a major center of clothing manufacture because of the presence of firms, such as H. Black & Co., Printz, Biederman Co., Landesman-Hirschheimer Co., and Goldsmith, Joseph & Feiss Co. The latter traces its beginnings to the 1860s to the firm of Koch & Loeb, which became Koch, Goldsmith, Joseph & Feiss Co. in 1873, and subsequently Goldsmith, Joseph Feiss & Co. ca. 1892 (Frank E. Joseph)

3. A knowledge of English and German was a selling point for a young man starting out in the work world in an immigrant community. This want ad appeared in the Cleveland *Plain Dealer*, May 13, 1882.

Ben F. Corday, at the extreme right, was one young man who found other employment outside the tobacco and clothing industries. About 1885 he became an apprentice at Jacob and Frank Strauss, printers, and subsequently established his own printing company of Corday and Gross. ca. 1885 (Mrs. Jacob Wattenmaker)

1.

2.

1. Emil Joseph (1857–1938) was one of the first American educated Jewish lawyers in Cleveland. He was active in civic and philanthropic affairs, including years of service on the Cleveland Library Board. He is shown, standing in the rear to the right of the pillar, with his fellow students at Columbia Law School. Theodore Roosevelt, a classmate, stands at the lower left. 1881 (Frank E. Joseph)

2. The law firm of Gilbert and Joseph opened its practice at 243 W. Superior, near the site of the Detroit-Superior bridge. ca. 1885 (Frank E. Joseph)

1. As the Jewish community grew, it established traditional social service institutions. In 1868 the fraternal
order of B'nai B'rith, Districts 2 and 6, selected Cleveland as the site of its home for orphan children of Jewish
Civil War veterans. They acquired Dr. Seelye's Water Cure
Sanitarium at Sawtell (E. 51st Street) and Woodland Avenue for the sum of $31,000, and rededicated it as the Jew-
ish Orphan Asylum. n.d. (Western Reserve Historical Society)

2. Abraham Hays (1794–1877) in Storndorf, Oberhessen,
first saw his children safely to the United States before
joining them in 1856 with the youngest member of the
family, Joseph. In the family photo, seated left to right,
are Belle Hays Oppenheimer, Abraham Hays, and Fannie Hays Klein; standing are Rosa Hays Loeb, Kaufman
Hays, Joseph Hays, and Yetta Hays Rohrheimer. ca. 1875
(Nancy Jacobs)

Jewish newcomers to the area also settled west of the Cuyahoga River. Samuel and Hannah Rickman established their business on Lorain Street; they pose here with their neighbors in front of their "gents" clothing store. ca. 1885 (Howard Klein)

1. Emigration often meant that aged parents and relatives were left behind, to be recalled in memory and occasionally by a photograph. The tintype of Simon and Hannah Joseph was sent to their son, Moritz, who came to Cleveland in 1873. ca. 1875 (Frank E. Joseph)

2. August F. "Gus" Hartz (1843–1929) stopped in Cleveland in 1879 as a touring magician and decided soon afterwards to stay. He was best known as a theatrical impresario and manager of the Euclid Avenue Opera House, owned by his friend, Marcus A. Hanna. (Cleveland *Plain Dealer*, January 13, 1879)

3. Jewish social life became more exclusive with the organization of the Excelsior Club in 1872 "for the promotion of the social and intellectual side of the Jew." Its first clubroom was in Halle's Hall on Superior Street opposite the old City Hall. In 1877 it was located in a new Halle building at the corner of Woodland and Erie (E. 9th) Streets. Members built the Excelsior Club at E. 38th Street and Woodland Avenue in 1887, where they remained until 1909. (Western Reserve Historical Society)

1.

2.

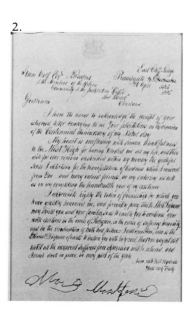

1. By 1880 there were approximately 3,500 Jews in Cleveland. Noting the growing number of aged, particularly among the early pioneer group, the fraternal order of Kesher Shel Barzel (The Bond of Iron) established the Kesher Home for Aged and Infirm Israelites in 1882 at Woodland and Willson (E. 55th Street) Avenues. ca. 1895 (Cleveland Public Library)

2. In 1884 the Kesher Home for Jewish Aged added the name of Sir Moses Montefiore, the English-Jewish philanthropist, on the occasion of his centennial birthday. A note of thanks and a gift of five pounds sterling to the Home acknowledged the tribute. (Montefiore Home)

Woodland

My childhood was spent in the slums of
Cleveland. Images appear, vanish, and re-
appear like the detailed patterns in tapestry
or colors spotted on a canvas in a correlated
design. The eye and mind wander over the
surface picking out details from the overall
pattern—a wide street with clanking
streetcars, trolley wires overhead; towards
evening, crowds coming home from work,
hanging like bees on a running board of the
trolleys. At dusk, wagons drawn by six gal-
loping horses; smells, kids yelling "ho, ho,
honey dumpers." Woodland Avenue, once a
beautiful, wide, tree-lined street with hand-
some houses—then a dilapidated slum,
a market street where farmers lined their
produce up along the sidewalks and cried
their wares. Across the street, houses seemed
a long way off, set in back of dried up lawns
full of tall dried grass and weeds. A small
boy seldom walked across the street.

*William Zorach describing lower
Woodland Avenue in the early 1900s.
From his autobiography, Art is My Life,
(1967); Quoted by permission of
Harper & Row, Publishers, Inc.*

Map of the Willson (E. 55th)-Woodland Avenues area. 1894 (Western Reserve Historical Society)

By 1895 the lower Woodland area, where Russian Jews first came to rest in their flight from persecution, was already being described as a slum. Its boundaries expanded as they pressed outward in ever growing numbers along Woodland, Scovill and Orange Avenues. Approximately 35,000 arrived in the city between 1905 and 1912, and the overcrowding was almost universal. The crush of housing can be sensed in this rooftop view from Hiram House at 27th Street and Orange Avenue. ca. 1910 (Western Reserve Historical Society)

1.

3.

1.   Many of the early homes in Woodland were originally built for single families. Later, as the pressure for housing exploded, three and four families shared the same dwelling. Sometimes, a house even became a synagogue. The sign in the photograph identifies the home of Congregation Anshe Galicia Minhag S'fard. Its members were predominantly from Polish Galicia, and its style of prayer derived from the Spanish Jews who reached there after their expulsion from Spain in 1492. ca. 1915 (Cleveland *Plain Dealer* Photo)

2.   Bathtubs were rare in the crowded lower Woodland district. One survey reported finding only one bathtub for every 600 homes in the area, with the result that Cleveland's first public bath house was erected in 1899 at 1611 Orange Avenue. ca. 1920 (Cleveland *Plain Dealer* Photo)

3.   When resources permitted, Jews emigrated from eastern Europe in family units. The family of Moshe Hirsch Wasser posed for a family portrait outside their *shtetl* home in the Vladimir-Volynsk region of eastern Poland. During the next seven years, Moshe Hirsch and the two infant children died, and the rest of the family—mother Feige, her three sons and two youngest daughters—left for the new world to change their lives and fortune. 1905 (Miriam Fisher)

1.

2.

3.

1. Case Avenue (E. 40th Street) in the 1880s and 1890s was the street of fashionable Woodland area homes. The Abraham Stearn residence, 1030 Case, typifies the style of the period. ca. 1900 (Mrs. Alan S. Geismer)

2. The interior of the Stearn home had a rich elegance. The noted Cleveland architect, Charles Schweinfurth, designed the fireplace mantel. ca. 1895 (Mrs. Alan S. Geismer)

3. As the community grew larger in numbers, Jewish society events were reported frequently in the local press and in even greater detail after establishment of the Anglo-Jewish press in 1889. This photograph of Rose Gleichman in her wedding gown at the time of her marriage to Emanuel Mandelbaum symbolizes Jewish social life in the late 19th century. 1893 (Sue H. Weiner)

A wedding anniversary was the occasion for celebration by the family of Joseph and Mathilda Garson assembled in their fashionable apartment at The Majestic on Willson Avenue (2291 E. 55th Street) ca. 1904–05 (Robert A. Garson)

Aaron Hahn, rabbi of the Reform Congregation Tifereth Israel (The Temple) from 1874–1892, remained a prominent figure in the Jewish community after leaving the pulpit to become a lecturer and, later, an attorney. He is seen here with family and relatives in his home at 1914 E. 66th Street. 1910 (Frank E. Joseph)

1.

3.

2.

1.   Abraham Wiener began his career as a grocery boy at age twelve in 1852. Within a decade he was known as the "boy commission merchant of Cleveland." By the 1890s Wiener Bros. & Co. was a major commission house in the region. Active in Jewish life, he was for years president of the Jewish Orphan Asylum. He is shown here with his wife and three children; the older girl is Ruth Wiener Einstein. 1897 (Paul Eden)

2.   Cleveland Jews began to enter the professions in small numbers in the second half of the 19th century. In medicine, Dr. Marcus Rosenwasser (1846–1910), who came here as an immigrant child, studied medicine in Europe and returned in 1868 to begin a notable career of service as an obstetrician, gynecologist and teacher. For a time, Dr. Rosenwasser had his office at his home on Woodland Avenue. ca. 1900 (Mrs. Norman Kyman)

3.   Besides buggy rides, picnics and occasional visits to Luna Park, cycling was another pleasant form of recreation. A group of girl cyclists prepare for their Sunday ride; Mary Grossman, later Judge, is at center right. 1899 (Edith Garver)

The Woodland district had its share of livery stables, and some homes, particularly of peddlers, had their own small barns. Before the horse gave way to the automobile, a buggy ride made a relaxed, pleasant afternoon for two ladies, Nettie Ullman (right) and her girlfriend. ca. 1895 (Rufus M. Ullman)

1.

2.

3.

1. When Congregation Anshe Chesed outgrew its Eagle Street home, it relocated in 1887 at E. 25th Street and Scovill Avenue. With the move the congregation took on a new popular name, the Scovill Avenue Temple. The sanctuary was described as magnificent—140 feet long and 72 feet wide, encircled by a gallery, with a seating capacity of 1,500. The photograph is from the cover of Anshe Chesed's golden anniversary book. 1896 (Fairmount Temple)

2. Whatever the differences then between Reform and Orthodox practices, holiday customs remained very much the same. Here young pupils in Queen Esther costumes celebrate the Purim holiday at the Scovill Avenue Temple. 1894 (Western Reserve Historical Society)

3. From 1876 to 1907 Michaelis Machol was rabbi of Scovill Avenue Temple. He is shown here, fourth from left, with a picnic group of congregational leaders. ca. 1898 (Cleveland *Jewish Society Book*, I)

1.

2.

1. Rabbi Aaron Hahn served the more Reform-minded Tifereth Israel congregation on Huron Road from 1874 to 1892, when he resigned. He was a popular speaker on religious and secular subjects and initiated a Sunday morning lecture series at The Temple. He stands at the left with a group of his school children. ca. 1887 (Cleveland *Jewish Society Book*, I.)

2. Moses J. Gries, rabbi of Congregation Tifereth Israel, 1892–1917, was the distinguished leader and spokesman of the Jewish community throughout his twenty-five years of service. ca. 1895 (Nancy Jacobs)

1.

2.

1. Interior of the Willson Avenue Temple. n.d. (American Jewish Archives, Cincinnati)

2. Two outstanding religious structures dominated the Willson-Woodland Avenue section. Designed by the architectural firm of Israel Lehman and Theodore Schmidt, the Willson Avenue Temple was dedicated by Congregation Tifereth Israel on September 21-24, 1894. Under the guidance of Rabbi Moses Gries, it quickly became a center of religious and cultural activities for the entire community. ca. 1900 (American Jewish Archives, Cincinnati)

1.

2.

1. The first Talmud Torah class in the new home of Congregation Oheb Zedek. Edward Heiser, who treasured the photograph, stands in the top row, second from the left. 1907 (Taylor Road Synagogue)

2. East European Orthodox immigrants entered into a pattern of institutional development similar to the early congregations. Although some joined the two mid-19th century congregations, B'nai Jeshurun (Temple on the Heights) and Anshe Emeth (Park Synagogue)—then Orthodox and decades later Conservative—many newcomers, once at home, established religious groups based on old country ties and styles of worship.

Congregation Oheb Zedek (Lovers of Righteousness), now part of Taylor Road Synagogue, built its facility at E. 38th Street and Scovill Avenue in 1905 at a cost of $42,000; it remained there until 1922. The building is now the Triedstone Baptist Church. 1974 (Richard E. Karberg)

1.

3.

1.   Congregation Anshe Emeth (People of Truth; later Park Synagogue) established in 1869 by Polish Jews, dedicated its house of prayer at E. 37th and Longwood in 1904. The congregation moved to the Glenville area in 1920; the former synagogue is now occupied by the Zion Hill Baptist Church. 1974 (Richard E. Karberg)

2.   Congregation Ohavei Emuna (Lovers of the Faith) was organized by Russian Jews in 1882, and became known as the "Russiche Shul" (synagogue). It was located on Hill Street (Haymarket) at the time its choir was photographed. ca. 1894 (Charles de Harrack)

3.   In 1906, Congregation B'nai Jeshurun (Temple on the Heights) moved from its Eagle Street synagogue, formerly the home of the Anshe Chesed congregation, to a new synagogue of Greco-Roman design topped by a Star of David; it was located at Willson and Scovill Avenues. The dedication ceremonies featured an address by Mayor Tom Johnson. ca. 1906 (Western Reserve Historical Society)

1.

2.

3.

A Happy and Prosperous New Year

1. During the Succoth holiday (Festival of Booths), observant families used what materials were at hand to construct a "succah" in which to have their meals and so recall the Biblical journey to freedom after the Exodus from Egypt. Abraham Bernstein used at least part of his attached storage room or barn for his construction. ca. 1910 (Martin E. Blum)

2. Congregational affiliation was always less than the numbers who wished to pray on the high holy days of the Jewish New Year. A cantor was the central figure in the services; here Cantor S. Talisman announces in a poster that he will officiate at the holiday services in the Royal Theater at 37th Street and Woodland Avenue. ca. 1915 (Mrs. Rose Breslauer)

3. Newcomer or citizen, poor or well-to-do, Jews of all circumstances were joined by faith in celebration of religious holidays. No holiday festival could be more appropriate in a free land than Passover, here observed by the Kritzer family at the *Seder* (Passover meal). ca. 1910 (Mrs. Morris K. Silverberg)

2.

1. Every block on Woodland Avenue had its cluster of neighborhood "mom and pop" businesses—groceries, confectioneries, butcher shops—in which the proprietors frequently lived in the rear of their stores or in apartments above them. The Kritzer family operated a number of bakery shops in the district, including this one by Nathan Kritzer at 2944 Woodland Avenue. The driver, third from left, is Abraham Sherwin, who went on to establish his own bakery. ca. 1907 (Louis Sherwin)

2. Bread was an important staple, and every baker took pride in the quality of his rye bread, keeping his recipe secret from his fellow members in the Jewish Bakers Union Local No. 50. Nathan Kritzer was one of this group of master bakers. 1899 (Mrs. Sol K. Marks)

No Sabbath meal was complete without a fish and chicken dinner with, of course, chicken soup. The Manheim poultry and fish store was located at 3226 Woodland Avenue. ca. 1910 (Dr. Sally Wertheim)

1. The Cleveland Consolidated Bottling Company was a predecessor of the Miller-Becker Company in the soft drink industry. Its plant served small beverage companies, such as that of Louis Gray (left rear), whose customers preferred his flavors and brand to those of his competitors. ca. 1898 (Alvin Gray)

2. Henry and Rose Roth pose with their children, Arthur and Irwin, outside their tailor shop at E. 38th and Central Avenue, another essential service for area residents. 1905 (Dr. Arthur A. Roth)

1.

2.

1. Some stores shared a common entrance and formed a natural side-by-side combination for more convenient daily shopping. Lamden and Fromson's delicatessen and Fine's grocery were close business neighbors at 3644 Woodland Avenue. ca. 1914 (Jack Kleinman)

2. The kosher butcher shop was another essential stop in neighborhood shopping. Frank Krasny trims a roast behind the counter of his market at E. 51st Street and Woodland Avenue. 1913 (Fay Siegel)

1. Willson Avenue marked the eastern end of the Woodland district, although people and shops spilled over down the streets past the main intersection. But the big transfer, when it came, was a jump into the Mt. Pleasant and Glenville areas. ca. 1900 (Western Reserve Historical Society)

2. The typical Woodland Avenue business block consisted of street level stores and second and, sometimes, third floor apartments. The 3800 block is the background in this photograph. 1908 (Mrs. David Schulman)

1.

2.

1. Scovill, Orange, Quincy, Central—these avenues paralleled Woodland and had similar neighborhood stores, although not as many per block. Sam Kaplan's Clothing and Pawn Shop, 4802 Scovill Avenue. ca. 1918 (Mrs. Milton Cohen)

2. Ignatz Klein's Hungarian restaurant at 736 Prospect Avenue was a favorite spot for special occasions. The restaurant was first located on Woodland Avenue. Possibly the growing presence of immigrants, who could little afford to eat out, even at the prices listed, made a move advisable. ca. 1909 (William A. Klein)

1.   Solomon Strauss enlisted at age 18 in the Fifth Ohio Volunteer Infantry during the Spanish American War. He served 53 days and was discharged, his service "honest and faithful." 1898 (Robert Strauss)

2.   The fraternal order of Knights of Pythias had its Jewish members in Cleveland clustered in Deak Lodge. Leon Baum, as his uniform and sword indicate, was one of its officers. ca. 1908 (Lillian Barrish)

1.

2.

1. Hy Rosenfeld's tailor shop, 59th Street and Quincy Avenue. ca. 1923 (Hilda Gladstone)

2. Peddling for East European Jews was not always the starting point to business success it proved to be for their 19th century predecessors. Many never worked their way up out of peddling or scavenging and continued to sell their wares along Woodland Avenue long after Jews had moved away. 1934 (*Friday Magazine*)

Woodland was not dominated by large tenements housing dozens of immigrant families. The overcrowding, a matter of concern to social welfare leaders, did not begin to match the immigrant ghettos of the eastern port cities, especially New York. Once they found their way, immigrant families often managed spare but relatively comfortable living quarters as this photo suggests. ca. 1912 (Edith Jaffe)

1.

2.

1.   Michael Frank sold religious books and wares in his store at 6001 Quincy Avenue. He was also a *sofer* (scribe), skilled in the writing and repair of religious documents. ca. 1917 (Aaron Frank)

2.   Some immigrant Jews were craftsmen trained in the old country. Blacksmith Isadore Teitelman came to Cleveland in 1910, opened his first shop on Scovill Avenue, and in 1933 moved his smithy to 3111 Woodland Avenue. 1938 (Sara E. Teitelman)

Dr. Arnold Peskind (1862–1944), born in Russia, was educated at Wooster Medical College in Ohio and at Jefferson Medical College in Philadelphia. He received his degree in medicine in 1886 and practiced medicine in Cleveland for 57 years. The portrait is by the well-known Cleveland photographer, Geoffrey Landesman. ca. 1940 (H. Jack Lang)

1.

2.

1. The Jewish carpenters in Cleveland were chartered in 1903 as Local 1750 of the United Brotherhood of Carpenters and Joiners. The Local's success in gaining higher wages for its members soon attracted almost all the eligible Jewish carpenters. It numbered about 200 members by 1911, when a contingent dressed in white overalls prepared to march from E. 37th and Woodland in the Labor Day parade. 1911 (Jewish Community Federation)

2. Jewish fraternal organizations, American rather than *landsmanshaft* in style, were another sign of adjustment to the new culture. Cleveland Lodge of the Order of B'nai B'rith was the first to be organized in 1850. The membership of the Order's several lodges established during the century was largely German Jewish. In the early 1900s, the Knights of Joseph attracted the newer immigrants. The Knights of Washington Lodge pose in parade dress, its officers in the front row; Major W.S. Rubinstein (fourth from the left), commanding. 1906 (*Jewish Independent*)

1. Everyone who could worked to supplement meager incomes in the immigrant family. Selling newspapers was one way to help out. Rivalry for selling corners was intense, particularly among ethnic groups, and Jewish newsboys organized a union in 1900 primarily for mutual protection. Two newsboys, Sam Givelber and Harry Sanger, had their corner near 55th Street and Woodland Avenue. ca. 1915 (Samuel H. Givelber)

2. Immigrant girls, once they mastered the sewing machine, found ready employment in the thriving garment industry. Other young ladies from earlier families added business skills to their knowledge of English and took secretarial jobs. Henrietta Salomon, a stenographer, sits at her typing desk at the Mugler Engraving Company. 1910 (Georgene Kravitz)

3. College education and training was a rarity in the immigrant culture pattern; that was to come later. Following school, one found a job or helped in the family enterprise as did Isadore Porubisky, who worked as a milkman for his father. Milk reached the Porubiskys' small dairy via interurban railway and was bottled for home delivery. ca. 1905 (Don Porbert)

1.

2.

1. Not every immigrant shared a vision of business success. Owning a small business meant security but lacked glamor and excitement. Sam Tuffyas, who came to the United States in 1908, sold men's furnishings in his store on West 25th Street, but his dream was to be a popular songwriter. ca. 1912 (Irving Tuffyas)

2. Tuffyas wrote a number of songs, "When I Lost My Dear Old Dad," "Sadie, Be a Lady and Write a Letter to Me," "I'll Never Spoon Beneath the Moon," and others. Some he published privately, but the doors of Tin Pan Alley failed to open. By 1920 he gave up his dream and became an insurance agent. 1914 (Irving Tuffyas)

2.

1. For Mortimer Greenberg a job as delivery boy was the way to start out in the work world. Although the May Company began truck service in 1901, horse and wagon remained a primary delivery service for a good number of years afterwards. 1908 (David H. Greenberg)

2. Job opportunities of higher status for teenagers possibly called for more ingrained American patterns and background. Born in Newark, New Jersey, George Freeman came to Cleveland after a prior family move to Mississippi. In his mid-teens, he obtained a job at the Postal Union and proudly posed in uniform with bicycle for a studio photograph. ca. 1917 (Mrs. Joyce Rothenberg)

1.

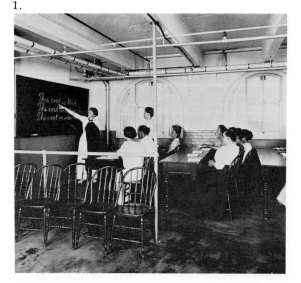

2.

3.

1. The clothing industry was a large-scale employer of immigrant labor. Necessary skills were often acquired in classes offered at settlement houses, special schools like the Cleveland Cutting School in the Woodland district, and on the job. At Joseph & Feiss, instruction in English, basic and business-related, was also part of the training for new employees. ca. 1915 (Joseph & Feiss)

2. Jacob Landesman, already making women's dusters and dresses in his own home, was joined by Felix Hirschheimer in 1880. They incorporated in 1896, and their company became one of the city's largest cloak manufacturers. The scene is the Landesman-Hirschheimer cutting and sewing room. ca. 1911 (Milton Sachs)

3. The Bloomfield Company, skirt and dress manufacturers, was established in 1904 and remained in business until sold in 1960. Here employees work on pleated skirts. ca. 1908 (Howard Bloomfield)

2.

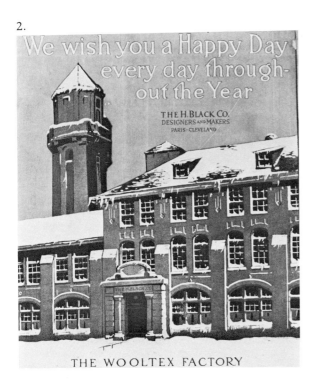

1. The pioneer firm of Koch, Goldsmith, Joseph & Company ultimately became Joseph & Feiss in 1907, one of the largest clothing concerns in the country. Its president, Paul L. Feiss, was a prominent civic leader for many years and an exponent of the scientific management movement. ca. 1910 (Joseph & Feiss)

2. In a survey in 1892 the *Plain Dealer* listed twenty-two local manufacturers and wholesale houses in the clothing industry, all of them Jewish. These firms for the next three decades made Cleveland a rival of New York. The H. Black Company, started in 1874, produced women's ready-to-wear cloaks and became a leading clothing manufacturer under the Wooltex label. The Black logo was inspired by the blizzard of November 10, 1913 (Western Reserve Historical Society)

1.

2.

3.

1. Jewish participation in the varied economic life of the community was not limited to the garment industry. It was recognized also in department store merchandizing, notably the Bailey Company (no longer in existence), Halle's and the May Company. The latter was established here in 1899 by the parent company located in Denver; in 1901 it located on Euclid Avenue on the south side near Public Square. ca. 1905 (Western Reserve Historical Society)

2. Cigar factories, such as Ology on West 3rd Street, employed the foreign-born in large numbers. A skilled workman in 1900 earned $11-12 for a 42-hour week. Joseph Newman's autobiography, *Smoke Dreams*, describes the growth of Cleveland's cigar industry. ca. 1915 (Jewish Community Federation)

3. A number of important Jewish businesses got their start during the Woodland era and became in time examples of the American success story. Harry Blonder began his rise in a small hardware store, 4408 Scovill Avenue, which grew into a major wallpaper and paint concern. 1913 (Erwin Blonder)

Commodore Louis D. Beaumont came to Cleveland to direct the new May Company branch. Although a Cleveland resident for less than a decade, he left a philanthropic legacy to the city in the Beaumont Foundation. The Commodore is shown here with his son and driver on a New York street. ca. 1905 (Robert D. Gries)

1. Charles Stein found a good location for his jewelry store on Ontario Street. Musical instruments also seemed to be part of his stock in trade. 1885 (Mrs. Arnold Aaron)

2. Joseph and Ben Salomon began their fuel supply company some time after 1900. When the "Model T's" took over, they erected one of the first gasoline stations in Cleveland, Keystone Oil Supply, later acquired by Standard Oil. ca. 1912 (Georgene Kravitz)

3. Harry Golden, a salesman for the S. M. Tobacco Company (S. Mechalowitz) made his sales calls and deliveries in a horse and wagon. He could be reached through either of two competing phone systems, Cuyahoga or Bell Telephone. 1914 (Louis Golden)

A different and more unusual enterprise was the trunk manufacturing business established by Isaac and Henry Feigenbaum at 1272 West 6th Street at the turn of the century. ca. 1912 (Mrs. Alex Estreicher)

Adolph Weinberger, founder of the national chain, Gray Drug, opened his original pharmacy at 3001 Scovill Avenue ca. 1914 (Gray Drug Company)

1.   Miller-Becker Company, today Cotton Club Beverages, started at the turn of the century when Coca-Cola was believed to be a health tonic. ca. 1910 (Jewish Community Federation)

2.   Cleveland grew rapidly in three decades from 93,000 residents in 1870 to 382,000 in 1900. Even though Jews were not found in heavy industry, which generated much of this growth, they were well represented in the increasing number of stores and business enterprises related directly to this population spurt. Louis S. Bing founded the Bing Furniture Company in 1891 and stored his furniture in this warehouse on West Superior. ca. 1892 (George Bing)

Another success story, one based on tradition and stability, began in 1886 when Jacob L. Goodman, front row center, opened his furniture store at Broadway and Harvard, not too distant from its present-day location. ca. 1900 (Henry L. Goodman)

A Mammoth Brewery.

1. Businesses in Woodland were usually modest, but occasionally there was promise of growth. Simon Fishel, who had been general manager of the Cleveland & Sandusky Brewing Company, announced plans to erect a $200,000 brewery in the district, which became the Forest City Brewing Co. 1906 (*Jewish Review and Observer*)

2. Immigrant distrust of banks turned enterprising saloon keepers into dealers in foreign exchange. They held—and used—immigrant patrons' savings until instructed to send money back to family in the old country or steam ship tickets so they could join those already in America.

   Henry Spira, who came to Cleveland about 1885 from Bartfeld, Hungary, opened a saloon several years later at 103 (renumbered 599) Broadway. His early foreign exchange department was located in front of the store and was partitioned from the saloon in the rear. ca. 1910 (Sig Spira)

1.

2.

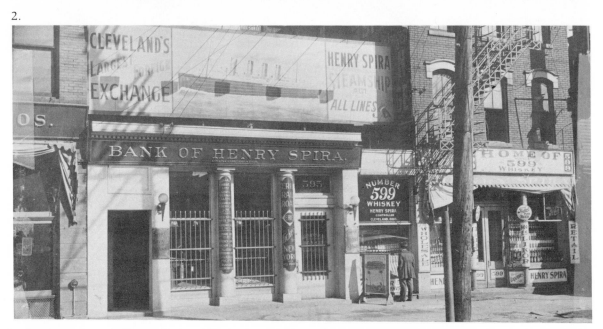

1.   Interior scene at the Foreign Exchange Bank. Henry Spira stands at the right. ca. 1910 (Sig Spira)

2.   Spira's Foreign Exchange Bank took on additional banking functions and became the Bank of Henry Spira. The immigrant bank was first located next to Spira's saloon and liquor business on Broadway and moved about 1916 to 31st and Woodland Avenue. In the 1920s it became part of the Guardian Trust Company and closed its doors permanently during the bank holiday of 1933. ca. 1915 (Sig Spira)

Education was valued by the newcomers who saw to it that their children took full advantage of the public school system. For the immigrant generation in the Woodland area, the classrooms of Brownell, Case-Woodland, Outwaithe, and Central High were their formal training grounds for American life. Newly arrived immigrant children of varying ages were often grouped together in a "steamer" class for English language instruction. This mix of pupils was photographed at South Case Elementary School, E. 40th and Central Avenue. 1911 (Sam Wohl)

1.

2.

3.

1.   Case-Woodland Elementary School at E. 40th and Woodland. ca. 1920 (Cleveland *Press*)

2.   A fifth grade class at Case-Woodland. ca. 1920. (Mrs. James Elsoffer)

3.   Another elementary school, Mayflower School, at the corner of E. 31st and Orange Avenue opened with two classrooms in 1852. By 1869 it had expanded to accommodate a thousand pupils. The school continued for years to introduce immigrant children to the basics of the English language. Pictured here is a second grade class in 1902. (Frances Turner)

1.

2.

3.

1. Basketball was a prime favorite among the games Jewish children played, to judge by the number of extant team photos. The "Terrors" are a representative team of young players; Allan Hexter (standing) and Sylvester Flesheim (second row right) went on to play varsity for Central High. 1904 (Sue H. Weiner)

2. The new Central High School with its clock tower opened its doors in 1878 at 2200 E. 55th Street. From 1900 to the early twenties, a high percentage of its students was Jewish, although not to the level reached by Glenville High School in a later period. ca. 1900 (Sara Louise Blum)

3. The graduating class of Central High School, showing the student look seventy years ago. 1908 (Frances Turner)

"And thou shalt teach them diligently to thy children." To parents religious instruction was equally important as public school education. Mindful of this imperative, the new immigrants began to organize Hebrew School classes. The leading figures were Aaron Garber and Dr. Joshua Flock, who merged their "improved" *heder* (classroom) with the Montefiore Talmud Torah or Hebrew Free School in 1907. Dr. Moses Garber (left) and Aaron Garber (right) flank their class at the E. 35th Street school. ca. 1908 (Mrs. David E. Clayman)

1.

2.

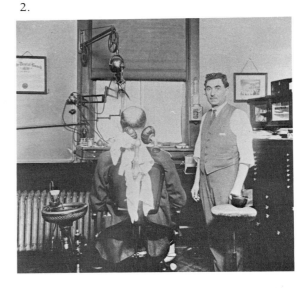

3.

1. The Talmud Torah climaxed its years in the Woodland area by acquiring a building at 2491 E. 55th Street, which it dedicated in 1921 to the memory of Rabbi Samuel Margolies, who was a prime mover in the Hebrew school movement until his death in 1917. (Cleveland Hebrew Schools)

2. Dr. Joshua Flock was a dentist by profession and divided his time between his practice and his passion for Hebrew education. ca. 1920 (Mrs. David Clayman)

3. Sometimes a family preferred private religious instruction, particularly in preparation for the Bar Mitzvah ceremony. The scene shows Harry and Hyman Baum with their *melamed* (teacher) and seems idyllic compared to the Hebrew classroom. ca. 1909 (Lillian Barrish)

The Zionist *Farband* (association), which combined commitment to the political Zionism of Theodore Herzl with socialist principles, was part of the culture Jews brought with them from Eastern Europe. It helped make Cleveland a center of the Zionist movement and the site for several national conferences. 1920 (Mrs. F. Kitner)

1.   Hebrew and Zionism were the keystones for special groups such as *Ha'Ivri Hatzair* (The Young Hebrew), whose objective was to encourage the study of modern Hebrew. 1915 (*Hadoar*, 1953)

2.   Cleveland was host to the 15th Annual Convention of the Federation of American Zionists in July, 1912. The Gesangverein Hall, at Scovill and Willson Avenues, was selected by the local leadership as the site for the meeting. 1912 (*Jewish Review and Observer*)

3.   Americans have been described as a nation of joiners. This impulse also influenced Orthodox Jewish women, whose honored and traditional role centered on her home and family. This role expanded, as evidenced by the founding convention in Cleveland in 1925 of the Mizrachi Women's Organization, a service and cultural association of Orthodox Jewish women. The background of the photograph shows the Hebrew Free Loan Association and the main branch of the Cleveland Hebrew Schools. 1925 (Mrs. Alex Estreicher)

לשנה טובה

A Happy New Year.

The Jewish Orphan Asylum or Home (now Bellefaire), situated on four acres of land at Sawtell (E. 51st Street) and Woodland Avenue, physically dominated the area through its complex of buildings and sheer size. Its children were never far from the eye and heart of the community. Author Edward Dahlberg, a resident from 1912 to 1917, described life there in exaggerated prose in *Because I Was Flesh*. But whatever its limitations and harshness in fact or memory, the Home had a high reputation as a model child care institution under the guidance of Dr. Samuel Wolfenstein, its superintendent for 35 years, 1878–1913. The main building of J.O.H. is framed in a Jewish New Year card. ca. 1895 (Western Reserve Historical Society)

1.

2.

1. A J.O.H. supervisor in his office, unidentified. ca. 1900 (Western Reserve Historical Society)

2. Dr. Samuel Wolfenstein, J.O.H. superintendent. ca. 1915 (Western Reserve Historical Society)

1.

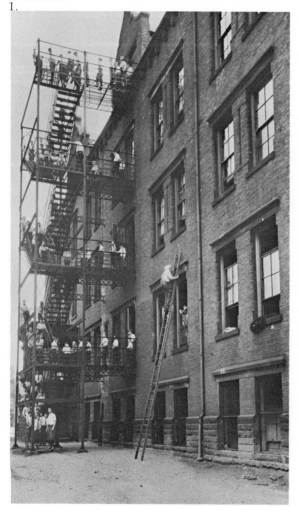

2.

1. The nucleus of the Home was the Water Cure Sanitarium purchased from Dr. Thomas Seelye in 1868. Its brick walls and iron fire escapes emphasized the solid qualities of the institution. ca. 1920 (Western Reserve Historical Society)

2. The Home awoke at 5:30 a.m. "In the washroom were two long soapstone troughs. Each boy, naked to the navel, his blue shirt, drawers and suspenders hanging, stood in front of a faucet, washed his face and body in icy water and scrubbed his teeth with Ivory soap." Edward Dahlberg. *Because I Was Flesh* (New Directions Publishing Company). Photo ca. 1915 (Western Reserve Historical Society)

Before they graduated from the Jewish Orphan Home, the boys and girls were taught useful skills. Here girls learn their way around a kitchen. ca. 1910 (Western Reserve Historical Society.

Boys learning auto mechanics on an Overland auto. ca. 1919 (Western Reserve Historical Society)

A girls' sewing class, ca. 1905 (Western Reserve Historical Society)

As part of their assigned housekeeping duties, boys fold and store clothes in the supply room. ca. 1915 (Western Reserve Historical Society)

1. Boy repairmen pose for a cameraman before starting on a job. ca. 1915 (Western Reserve Historical Society)

2. "Everybody wore the orphan asylum mouse-gray jackets, lank, straight pants that fell as far as the knees and woolen stockings with thick ridges." Edward Dahlberg. *Because I Was Flesh* (New Directions Publishing Company). The J.O.H. clothes style is clearly seen in this family photo to be treasured by a sorely missed parent. ca. 1905 (Western Reserve Historical Society)

1.

2.

1. On occasion, a parent visiting his children would preserve the moment in a photograph that suggests the problems that made separation necessary. ca. 1910 (Western Reserve Historical Society)

2. There was time for play at J.O.H. Boys with crew-cuts in asylum uniforms display toys most likely received from J.O.H. trustees on a holiday or school visit. ca. 1900 (Western Reserve Historical Society)

Baseball on J.O.H. grounds near the stable. ca. 1910 (Western Reserve Historical Society)

Practicing eurythmics outdoors on the J.O.H. front lawn. ca. 1915 (Western Reserve Historical Society)

The Home provided its own entertainment with young musicians. ca. 1920 (Western Reserve Historical Society)

In the last quarter of the 19th century women began to form groups which combined social needs with charitable purposes. The Young Ladies Charitable Union (1875), Daughters of Charity (1892) and The Willing Workers (1893), among others, set themselves tasks to assist poor and needy immigrants. The Busy Bee Society, pictured here, organized about 1889 and sponsored benefits which were also social occasions for their circle of friends. Mrs. Abraham Wiener stands in front of the hive. ca. 1890 (Paul Eden)

1.

2.

ENTERTAINMENT
Benefit the Sick Poor.
LITTLE BUSY BEES' SOCIETY
1082 Case Ave., Dec. 28, '93.

1. TABLEAU.
THE BUSY BEES, ... By the Entire Society.
2. RECITATION.
MARMION AND DOUGLAS, ... Samson Selig.
3. FARCE.
—THE FOUR CELEBRATED CHARACTERS—
LITTLE RED RIDING HOOD, . . . Florence E. Goodhart.
CINDERELLA, ... Gertrude Steinfelt.
SLEEPING BEAUTY, ... Helen J. Einstein.
GOLD SPINNER, ... Sophie Koppel.
4. RECITATION.
A TROUBLESOME CALL, ... Fanny Aub.
5. HOOP DRILL.
Elsie Klein, Mollie Stearn, Faith E. Russell, Florence Goodhart, Ida
Schwab, Helen L. Einstein.
6. RECITATION.
FINGERS OF FATE, ... Samson Selig.
7. FARCE.
"IS IT GOOD TO EAT?"
KATE, ... Ruth Wiener.
LOUISA, ... Faith Russell.
MARY, ... Mollie Stearn.
FLORA, ... Ida Schwab.
LUCY, ... Elsie Klein.
8. TABLEAU.—IN TWO PARTS.
I. HEADS. . . . . . II. TAILS.
9. STEREOPTIC EXHIBITION.

1.   The Council Educational Alliance, organized in 1897 "to engage in educational and philanthropic work" was first housed on lower Woodland Avenue, where its activities expanded rapidly. When the Excelsior moved to more fashionable quarters, the CEA in 1908 took over the club building, located at 3754 Woodland Avenue. The agency remained there until 1924 when it in turn moved to Kinsman Avenue and sold the property to the Friendly Inn. ca. 1920 (Western Reserve Historical Society)

2.   The list of participants in a Busy Bee social in 1893 included members of the social elite in the Jewish community. (Jewish Community Federation)

1.

2.

3.

1.   The Woodland CEA helped Americanize a generation of Jewish immigrants. For them—not for the native-born Jewish community—it was the center of Jewish life, vitalized in a whirl of classes, meetings, clubs, games and social events to the mixed sounds of Yiddish and accented English. This photo of an exercise class also suggests the interior elegance of the former Excelsior Club. ca. 1915 (Western Reserve Historical Society)

2.   Night classes for instruction in English, citizenship, homemaking, and crafts were attended by immigrants after a day's work. 1907 (*Jewish Independent*)

3.   Lower Woodland Avenue over the years began to show its wear and tear in run-down housing and littered alleys, which became the playgrounds for immigrant and under-privileged youth. ca. 1910 (Western Reserve University)

Class of 1920 -   Council Educational Alli

The CEA provided religious instruction with the help of local rabbis. Rabbi Solomon Goldman, then of congregation *B'nai Jeshurun*, confirmed the CEA class of 1920. (Western Reserve Historical Society)

1.

2.

Cleveland, Ohio, November 24, 1903.

The undersigned being all the trustees duly elected of The Federation of the Jewish Charities of Cleveland, hereby waive notice of the first meeting of said trustees and agree that said meeting may take place forthwith at the office of Emil Joseph, Society for Savings Building, Cleveland, Ohio, for the election of officers and such other business as may properly come before said meeting.

1.   By the mid-1890's larger Jewish communities had developed a variety of voluntary welfare agencies to assist with the problems posed by the enormous influx of East European Jews. The Jewish federation movement is based on Judaic traditions of *Tzedakah* (charity), a sense of communal responsibility, and a conviction that only by joining together would the thousands of newcomers be helped. Boston in 1895 organized the first Jewish federation in the United States. Cleveland leaders and representatives of seven local agencies began planning a similar organization in 1900, with Martin A. Marks of the Jewish Orphan Home as chairman of the organizing committee. Charles Eisenman, a businessman with a high sense of social responsibility, took a leading role in organizing the Cleveland Federation. He was its president from 1903 until his death in 1923; he is seated right with Federation leaders. Directly behind him is Samuel Goldhamer, director of the Federation from 1907–1948. 1912 (Jewish Community Federation)

2.   By 1903, the agencies reached an agreement for combined fund raising, and the trustees of the new Federation of Jewish Charities (today the Jewish Community Federation) held their first meeting on November 24, 1903. Their subscription list by the end of the year totaled 685 subscribers, who contributed $35,072. (Jewish Community Federation)

Form No. 260.

THE WESTERN UNION TELEGRAPH COMPANY.
——INCORPORATED——
23,000 OFFICES IN AMERICA.   CABLE SERVICE TO ALL THE WORLD.
ROBERT C. CLOWRY, President and General Manager.

Receiver's No.	Time Filed		Check

SEND the following message subject to the terms on back hereof, which are hereby agreed to.   Cleveland   June 22 1906

Speaker Cannon
   House of Representatives
   Washington D C

    The Federation of Jewish Charities representing the Jewish
community of Cleveland earnestly request that you use your influence
for the defeat of the immigration bill at present before Congress.
We are opposed to any literacy test, property qualification or increase in head tax. We furthermore deem it essential and just that
no bill be passed that does not contain an exemption clause similar
to that contained in the British Aliens Bill.

             E M Baker

                                    Secretary

☞ READ THE NOTICE AND AGREEMENT ON BACK. ☜

SUPPOSE THE SENATE REFUSES TO CONCUR IN THE HOUSE AMENDMENTS?

Uncle Sam.—I am sorry for you, my good woman, but you haven't the price of admission

—Drawn for The Jewish Independent

1.   Although fund raising and distribution of funds were the primary functions of the Federation of Jewish Charities in its early years, it soon became a central voice on broad issues of Jewish concern. In this instance, Federation protested a proposed literacy test in an immigration bill under consideration in the House of Representatives. 1910 (Jewish Community Federation)

2.   Legislation to restrict immigration, despite pogroms in Eastern Europe, impelled the local *Jewish Independent* to print one of its rare editorial cartoons. 1910 (*Jewish Independent*)

1.

2.

1. The tradition of providing help to those in need was accepted by the community, even if some of its members would have preferred the new immigrants to settle elsewhere. To help with family problems, community leaders organized the Hebrew Relief Association in 1875, which provided material aid on appeal. Professional casework services started in 1904 with the hiring of A. S. Newman. In 1907, Morris and Joseph Glauber donated a two-story frame house on Case Avenue (2554 E. 40th Street); it was dedicated in memory of their brother as the Isaac N. Glauber Memorial House. 1910 (*Jewish Review and Observer*)

2. Martin A. Marks (1853–1916), a success in the clothing trade and then as a general manager for Equitable Life, was most active in Jewish and general community affairs. President of Tifereth Israel for 23 years and a founder of the Federation of Jewish Philanthrophies, he used the latter as a model in guiding the formation of Cleveland's Federation for Charity and Philanthropy in 1913, now the Federation for Community Planning. ca. 1895 (Nancy Jacobs)

1.

2.

3.

1. Samuel D. Wise provided temporary relief from urban congestion for "children of all ages, working girls and boys, mothers with babes; and men and women, who are worn out and failing in health." In 1907, Wise donated property on Lake Erie, fifteen miles east of Cleveland near interurban railway Stop 133, as a summer camp. Camp Wise, now part of Halle Park, was dedicated in 1907 and staffed mainly by camp leaders from socially prominent families.

In the photograph, left to right are Walter Weil, Eugene Geismer, "Zook" Moss, Abel Warshawsky, Samuel Wise, Hilda Muhlhauser, Mrs. Wise, Mollie Stearn, Babette Moss, Mrs. Edgar Hahn, and Lilly Sloss. 1907 (David Warshawsky)

2. A play scene at the first Camp Wise. ca. 1915 (Western Reserve Historical Society)

3. Camp Wise in its early years was distinctly a contribution to the social welfare of immigrant children and attracted capable young socialites like Hilda Muhlhauser, who were very likely inspired by Jane Addams and Lillian D. Wald. 1908 (*Jewish Review and Observer*)

1.

2.

1. Swimming in Lake Erie, long before the dangers of pollution, was a popular activity at Camp Wise. The Woodland Avenue campers were not concerned about stylish swimming costumes. ca. 1915 (Western Reserve Historical Society)

2. Camp Wise cottages. c.a. 1915 (Western Reserve Historical Society)

1. The limited facilities of the original Camp Wise made it desirable to relocate the camp on a larger site near Painesville, where it opened for its 1927 summer season. It remained there 40 years until 1967, when it began operations in a new camp at the Jewish Community Center's Halle Park in Burton, Ohio. Near the main building was the huge "Front Rock", a meeting point for camping friends. ca. 1930 (Western Reserve Historical Society)

2. A milk break at one of the units at the new Camp Wise. ca. 1930 (Western Reserve Historical Society)

3. Pity the working girl. John Anisfield, a pioneer clothing manufacturer and philanthropist, made a gift about 1925 of a summer camp, which had been leased to the Jewish Girls Business Vocation Club organized ten years earlier. The camp grounds were near Huron, west of Cleveland, on Lake Erie. Shown is a group of Jewish business girls and friends at the summer camp site. The photographer was M. Herbert Wolf, who later became an attorney and occasional novelist. ca. 1915 (Muriel Rivchun)

1.

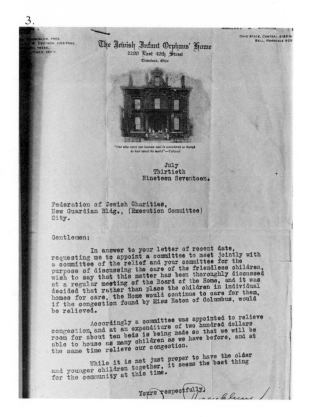

2.

3.

1. As East European immigrants crowded into Woodland, the early German-Jewish residents began to move out, and some of their homes became service centers for the newcomers. In 1903, the Women's Jewish Hospital Society purchased such a home (2371 E. 37th Street), which was the forerunner of Mt. Sinai Hospital. ca. 1910 (Mt. Sinai Hospital)

2. A second residence was acquired later at 2433 E. 55th Street and converted into the Mt. Sinai dispensary. ca. 1912 (Mt. Sinai Hospital)

3. Originally owned by Jacob Goldsmith, clothing manufacturer, this residence became the Jewish Infant Orphans' Home in 1908. The care center moved to the Glenville area in 1922. The building today houses the Universal Negro Improvement Association. ca. 1908 (Jewish Community Federation)

---

1. 173

2.

1. East European immigrants took root quickly in the Cleveland Jewish community and began to create their own institutions. One of the first was the Jewish Orthodox Home for Aged established in 1906 at 5912 Scovill Avenue. Its Orthodox orientation is seen in these two photographs. Residents pose outside the Home. ca. 1912 (Bernice Silverstein)

2. A glass slide shows men at prayer. ca. 1910 (Menorah Park)

1.

2.

1. The *landsmanshaft*, a fraternal organization set up on old country geographical lines, was an important supporting factor in the adjustment of Jewish immigrants to the American life style. Several of them continue to exist for benevolent and social purposes, such as the Brisker-Grodner Society. 1920 (Lillian Stein)

2. Pioneer Cleveland Jewish families were part of the community's social elite. The names of Thorman, Alsbacher, Hays, Hoffman and Rosenwasser, for example, appeared frequently in the social news. Isaac Hoffman, shown here with his children, was the son of Simson Hopferman, one of the original Unsleben group. ca. 1905 (Mrs. James L. Hoffman)

Headed by George Bellamy, Hiram House at 27th and Orange Avenue opened in 1899 in the midst of the Jewish community. The event shocked parents who feared that the settlement house would proselytize their children. ca. 1906 (Western Reserve Historical Society)

Despite warnings that they would be led astray, many Jewish immigrants and youngsters participated in Hiram House programs and activities. At least seven of the members in this photograph of the Social Reform Club are Jewish. One of them, Manuel Levine, seated second from left, gained prominence as a Cleveland judge. ca. 1914 (Western Reserve Historical Society)

1. On holidays—July 4th, Columbus Day—Woodland Avenue was the scene of Hiram House celebrations. Residents, Jews included, line the street in anticipation of the parade as the band assembled. ca. 1910 (Western Reserve Historical Society)

2. Interior of the Perry Street Theater, the second early home of Yiddish theater in Cleveland; it had a seating capacity of 900. A reporter at its opening wrote glowingly that "classic Hebrew drama has now a home in Cleveland that is worthy of its historic glories." ca. 1910 (Cleveland *Plain Dealer* Photo)

1.

H. R. JACOBS' CLEVELAND THEATER.
H. R. JACOBS............Sole Proprietor and Manager.
The only Theater playing Sterling Attractions at Popular Prices.
EVERYBODY GOES TO H. R. JACOBS' CLEVELAND THEATER.
Matinees Tuesday, Wednesday, Friday and Saturday. Last week of the regular season.
—This afternoon at 2—This Evening at 8—CHARLES McCARTHY in—

"One of the Bravest."

H. R. JACOBS' CLEVELAND THEATER.
H. R. JACOBS............Sole Manager and Proprietor.
SUNDAY EVENING, June 3. One Performance Only.
THE ROUMANIAN OPERA COMPANY
In the Great Historical Opera
BAR COCHBA | The Last Hour of Jerusalem.
The Prima Donna, Madame A. FINKEL, Supported by Max Avramovitz and Full Company.
Admission—25, 35, 50, 75, $1.

AT DEATH'S DOOR.

The End at Hand in General Sheridan's Case.

2.

3.

1.   Between 1905 and 1912 the influx of Jews from Russia and Poland increased the size of the community, from 25,000 to 60,000. The newcomers injected their "shtetl" values and created a new Woodland style—a mix of Yiddish, Hebrew and English, with strong Zionist commitments, adapted to an expanding American culture base. The appearance of Yiddish road shows in Cleveland in the late 1880s heralded the impending change. ca. 1888 (Cleveland *Plain Dealer* Photo)

2.   Yiddish theater found a home in Cleveland with the construction in 1901 of the Perry Street (E. 22nd) theater at the corner of Woodland Avenue. Known as "Bernstein's Block," after owner Harry Bernstein, the building also included a saloon, a bank and the Perry Hotel. ca. 1906 (Mrs. David Schulman)

3.   The dominant political figure in the immigrant community was Republican ward leader and councilman Harry Bernstein (1856-1920), popularly known as the "Czar of Woodland Avenue." He was the immigrant's friend, good for a small handout if in need, help if in difficulty with the law and always the advice to vote Republican. ca. 1900 (Mrs. David Schulman)

Bernstein transferred his base of operations from Perry Street to the People's Theater at 3718 Woodland Avenue about 1906. The theater offered Yiddish vaudeville and drama and the latest entertainment, the motiongraph. The "Czar" was always recognizable by his hat and a massive watch chain resting on an ample waist. The photograph includes Philip Weisenfreund (fourth from left), actor and father of Paul Muni. ca. 1908 (Mrs. David Schulman)

1.

2.

1. Typical of the Yiddish theatrical groups which came to Cleveland in 1910 was the Hart Company. The banner announces their play, "The White Slaves," written, produced and acted by Mr. and Mrs. Hart. The title, at least, recalls Bartley Campbell's post-Civil War play, "The White Slave." The photograph was taken in 1914, but not in Cleveland. (Jack Kleinman)

2. The Wonderland Theater at E. 9th and Superior Avenue started as a nickelodeon run by Max Lefkowitch (right). As this new entertainment industry grew, he expanded his business to operate a chain of theaters in the Cleveland area. ca. 1908 (Leo Greenberger)

1. Yiddish theater was strengthened by the loyal support of local devotees, many of whom would have preferred acting to their workaday jobs. Realistically, they continued to earn their bread in other ways and organized the Literary and Dramatic Union of the United States and Canada, which held its first convention in Cleveland at the Woodland Public Library, May 27-28, 1917. It marks the beginning of Jewish community theater in the city. (Sam Neshkin)

2. The star system, which made theatrical costs more reasonable, allowed members of the Literary and Dramatic Union to play supporting roles to visiting guest stars. This play bill, the first under the new system, announces the appearance of Jacob Ben Ami in Ossip Dimov's play, "The Hired Groom," at the Globe Theater. The local supporting cast included, among others, Joseph Feder, Sam Neshkin, and Anna Leit. May 29, 1918 (Sam Neshkin)

1.

2.

3.

1. Picnicking was a popular way to spend a Sunday afternoon in a less hurried age. Many young people found it particularly pleasant to leave the crowded streets of Woodland for a day to enjoy the open air of Edgewater Park. 1912 (Earl M. Linden)

2. The automobile put a nation on wheels and in its early years made a family weekend ride, especially with the top down, a pleasurable and mildly exciting occasion. Joseph Karp and family are ready to roll in their 1908 Royal. ca. 1910 (Morton E. Karp)

3. Auto or horse and buggy, life for most area residents moved on foot. They rode the trolley to work, but they walked to the stores to shop, to meetings, and to prayer. On Jewish holidays they strolled the avenues in their finery. This tranquil moment was recorded at E. 40th and Woodland Avenue. ca. 1904 (Cleveland *Plain Dealer*)

JOSEF ROSENBLATT, *Tenor*

Assisted by STUART ROSS, *at the Piano*

CLEVELAND, OHIO

January 23, 1919

Program

1　Aria, Pearl Fishers . . . . *Bizet*

2　Ov Horachmim }
　　Omar rabbi Elosor } . . . . *Josef Rosenblatt*

3　Piano Solos
　　　Prelude, E minor }
　　　Rondo Capriccioso } . . . . *Mendelssohn*
　　　　　　　Mr. ROSS

4　Elegie . . . . *Massenet*
　　Eili Eili . . . . *Arr. by Rosenblatt*

5　Piano Solos
　　　The Lark . . . . *Balakirew*
　　　Octave-Etude . . . . *Chopin*
　　　　　　　Mr. ROSS

6　Lullaby . . . . *Gretchaninoff*
　　Auf dem Pripichuk . . . . *Folksong*
　　La Danza . . . . *Rossini*

Steinway Piano Used

1.　Many Jewish artists, actors and musicians, stopped in Cleveland on tour. Jacob Adler, the tragedian, was sure to perform to full houses when he appeared here. But one of the more unique performances was the recital by Cantor Josef Rosenblatt under the musical direction of Adella Prentiss Hughes, founder of the Cleveland Orchestra. "Yoselle" of the golden voice had spurned an operatic career because of his religious Orthodoxy, but in concert he displayed his talent in a combined classical and cantorial program. January 23, 1919 (Jewish Community Federation)

2.　Max Apple, mandolin, started working at age ten in the old country. The family came to Cleveland in 1912, and here he had the opportunity for both schooling and music lessons. 1918 (Max Apple)

The sound of pianos in Jewish homes reflected not only a love of music but also improved circumstances since the day "Momma and Poppa" first arrived. Sam Solomon, composer of Yiddish songs and orchestra leader at the Globe and Duchess theaters, also taught piano. The cost: $1.50 per lesson. ca. 1920 (Mrs. Jack Finkelstein)

1.

He Will Advocate The Matrimonial Union Of Jew and Gentile

AUTHOR ABROAD GATHERING MATERIAL

Jesus Will Be The Central Figure In a Future Story—A Satirical Work on Foreign Noblemen In Preparation

Intermarriage of Jew and Gentile will be the theme of Ezra Brudno's next story for which the young Cleveland author is now gathering material abroad. Intimate friends of the author who know

other and more important work which he hopes will prove to be his masterpiece. In this work he will expound the teachings of Jesus, build a story around his times and in narrative form, speculate upon the significance of this historic event.

Mr. Brudno is now in Paris where he has been for some time acquiring a knowledge of French and carefully studying French customs and manners. Incidentally when he finds a few leisure moments he is engaged on the outlines of his Intermarriage story, which will be ready for publication in November.

The other book referred to above, is written in a humorous vein and is named "Baron Fritz." This work is already in shape for the press, and since Mr. Brudno's departure for Europe arrangements have been perfected for its dramatization.

"Baron Fritz" satirizes American society. The theme is the marketable value of titled foreigners and the prices they bring in this country among the ambitious millionaires with marriageable daughters whose fond papas and

2.

3.

ROSE HARRIET PHELPS STOKES

1. Ezra Brudno (1877-1936) was Cleveland's first Jewish novelist. An immigrant child, he was educated at Harvard Law School and wrote a number of novels with Jewish themes and characters. His best novel, *The Tether*, deals with the cultural clash between immigrant parents and their Americanized son, who still could not find social acceptance. Brudno by 1920 gave up writing novels to devote full time to his law practice. 1906 (*Jewish Independent*)

2. Yiddish litterateurs were also part of the East European wave which flowed into Cleveland. Shiah Miller wrote several novels, and one, unpublished, had Woodland Avenue with some of its personalities thinly disguised as background. Miller (left) poses with an artist friend; both wear banners asking for Purim gifts for war children. ca. 1919 (Sonia Rubinstein)

3. Two women captured the heart and imagination of the Jewish community during its Woodland period. One, Rose Pastor (1879-1933), brought romantic hope to those girls who had rolled cigars beside her in Gleichman's tobacco factory. In a variation on "Abie's Irish Rose," she moved on to a career as a journalist in New York, where she met and married millionaire J. Phelps Stokes; they were later divorced. Rose Stokes continued to write and be active in radical politics for many years. 1906 (*Jewish Independent*)

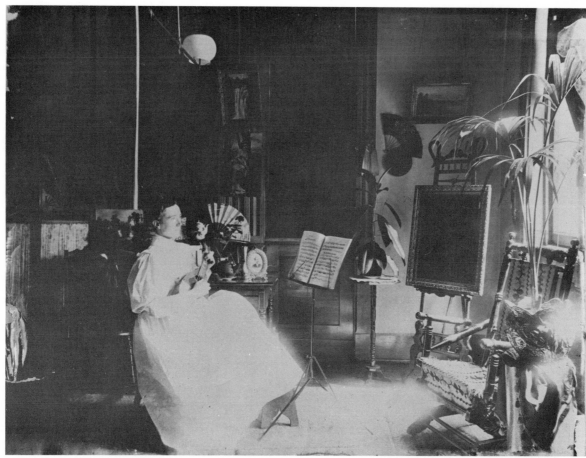

The second woman, Martha Wolfenstein (1869–1906), the daughter of Dr. Samuel Wolfenstein of the Jewish Orphan Home, was a writer. Her novel, *Idylls of the Gass* (The Alley), was set in the Austrian ghetto. It was published in 1901 and serialized in the local Anglo-Jewish press. Her devotion to the arts and her frailty because of tuberculosis are captured in this parlor setting. ca. 1900 (Jewish Community Federation)

A Statement of Aims and Principles

To provide the Jewish community of Greater Cleveland with a quality weekly newspaper which will fully present local, national, and world news of Jewish interest.

To offer commentary, interpretation, and authentic background on events of the day, as a means of stimulating the concern and response vital to the fulfillment of our responsibilities as Americans and as Jews.

To enrich the cultural life both of individuals and the community through the presentation of features, articles, reviews, and other material of Jewish content and interest.

To provide a forum for comment by members of the community wishing to express their viewpoints on matters of Jewish interest.

Cleveland Jewish News
October 30, 1964

The need to communicate within a Jewish community, which grew from about 3,500 in 1880 to 25,000 in 1905, led to efforts to establish an Anglo-Jewish newspaper. The *Hebrew Observer*, published by Hiram Straus and Sam Oppenheimer, was first on the scene in 1889. The *Plain Dealer* reported its new colleague "will be devoted to news and gossip of particular interest to Israelites." (Western Reserve Historical Society)

The *Jewish Review*, published by Jack Machol and Sam Oppenheimer, who had severed his ties with the *Observer*, appeared in 1893. (Western Reserve Historical Society)

Dan S. Wertheimer purchased the *Review* in 1896, and three years later merged it with the *Hebrew Observer*. The Wertheimer family published *The Jewish Review and Observer* until its final edition on October 23, 1964. (Western Reserve Historical Society)

Competition began for the *Review and Observer* in 1906, when Maurice Weidenthal, a local journalist, founded *The Jewish Independent*. (Western Reserve Historical Society)

1.

2.

1. The tremendous influx of Yiddish speaking East European Jews sparked early efforts to create a Yiddish press. The first to survive for any length of time, about two years, was *The Daily Press* founded in 1908 by Samuel Rocker. (Western Reserve Historical Society)

2. In 1917, Leo Weidenthal became editor-publisher of *The Jewish Independent* and until his retirement in 1964 was a respected and influential voice within the Jewish community. 1964 (Cleveland *Jewish News*)

The home of the Yiddish press was the Rocker Printing Company at E. 14th and Woodland Avenue. Publisher Samuel Rocker stands at the right. ca. 1902 (Judy Glickson)

1.

2.

3.

1. In 1911, Samuel Rocker returned to the newspaper field to publish and edit *Die Yiddishe Velt* (The *Jewish World*) as a weekly and later as a daily. In its final years, it became again a weekly. 1922 (Judy Glickson)

2. *Die Yiddishe Velt* was the voice of the East European Jewish community. For the next three decades it reflected their interests in contrast to the German-Jewish orientation of the Anglo-Jewish press. It ceased publication in 1952 as Yiddish succumbed to English in Jewish households. The headline in this 1913 issue proclaims "Beilis Innocent" in the infamous 20th century Passover blood libel case. (Western Reserve Historical Society)

3. Following in the wake of the Jewish population shift out of Woodland, the publisher of *Die Yiddishe Velt* moved his newspaper shop to the Glenville area at 10600 Superior. It remained there until the shop closed permanently. 1930 (Cleveland Board of Zoning Appeals)

1.

2.

1.   Opposition to *Yiddishe Velt* policies, much of it within the Orthodox Jewish community, led to the brief appearance in 1923 of *Die Yiddishe Waechter* (*The Jewish Guardian*), a Yiddish-English language weekly. Rabbi Samuel Benjamin was its managing editor. (Western Reserve Historical Society)

2.   To provide readership for their newspaper venture, the backers of *The Jewish Guardian* held a mass meeting and concert in the Woodland district October 11, 1922. However, even enthusiasm could not overcome the fact that the community lacked the readers to support two local Yiddish newspapers. 1922 (Western Reserve Historical Society)

1. Leon Wiesenfeld, a journalist in Prague, came to Cleveland via New York in 1925. Here he joined the staff of *Die Yiddishe Velt* but left in 1938 to start his own Yiddish-English newspaper, *Die Yiddishe Stimme—The Jewish Voice*. It ceased publication within a year for want of readers and advertisers. ca. 1937 (Mrs. Leon Wiesenfeld)

2. Masthead of *Die Yiddishe Stimme*, which indicates a national ambition never achieved. (Western Reserve Historical Society)

3. Translation. The English side of the weekly, *The Jewish Voice*. (Western Reserve Historical Society)

1.

2.

1.   Wiesenfeld next published *The Jewish Voice Pictorial*, which appeared annually at the start of the Jewish New Year. The cover of the 1954 edition featured Commodore Uriah Levy to commemorate the tercentenary of Jewish settlement in America. (Western Reserve Historical Society)

2.   *Friday* was a monthly magazine to which young writers contributed brief articles on local Jewish activities and issues. Published by Sam Abrams and edited by Elmer Louis, *Friday* first appeared in March, 1934, and survived for ten issues. (Western Reserve Historical Society)

The Cleveland Jewish News

The Weekly Newspaper for The Jewish Community of Greater Cleveland

Circulation This Issue: 19,692

Vol.—No. 1   FRIDAY, OCTOBER 30, 1964 — 24th of Heshvan, 5725   CLEVELAND, OHIO   62   10c per copy, $4 per year

'Moslem Manipulations' at UN Sharply Protested

By The Jewish Telegraphic Agency

UNITED NATIONS, N. Y. —Israel lodged a sharp protest this week with the chairman of the latest and largest bloc of United Nations members, the so-called "Group of 77" of developing countries, for being excluded from a meeting of the group Tuesday morning and for "unworthy strategems and manipulations" which were employed to keep Israel out of the group.

The protest was sent in a letter from Michael Comay, Israel's permanent representative here, to Syed Amjad Ali, of Pakistan, chairman of the Group of Developing Countries. The group consists of 77 Afro-Asian delegations, including Arab states, and Latin American representatives.

Mr. Ali had announced last week that a full-scale meeting of the entire group would be held Tuesday afternoon. However, upon the insistence of the Arab bloc and fellow-Moslem members, Mr. Ali suddenly called the group to a meeting that morning without inviting Israel. The right of Israel to full membership in the group was to have been on the agenda of the meeting originally scheduled Tuesday afternoon.

"I did not attend the meeting which took place this morning," Mr. Comay wrote to Mr. Ali, "because of the short notice at which the time was changed.

"However, to avoid any misunderstanding, I wish to state categorically that we shall continue to exercise our right to participate in the work of the group, and I must formally request that we be given full facility to do so, including notification of meetings, and any change in their time and place.

"There can be no bona fide and objective ground for our exclusion from the group," Mr. Comay continued. "The unworthy strategems and manipulations to which we have been subjected have nothing to do with the merits of our status in the group, but reflect the pursuit of political aims in a context in which they should have no place.

"It is our intention to participate as a matter of course in the next meeting of the group, and I would be obliged if you would inform me in advance when that meeting takes place."

The Jewish News will honor all unexpired subscriptions to the Jewish Independent and the Jewish Review & Observer. At the termination of the subscription, the reader will be billed by The News at the rate of $4 a year, with an option of a three-year subscription at the rate of $10.

STORMY EIGHT-HOUR MEETING BRINGS BACKING FOR PRIME MINISTER

Eshkol Scores Victory in Mapai Over Ben-Gurion on Alignment

TEL AVIV — Prime Minister Levi Eshkol emerged victorious Tuesday morning from a turbulent eight-hour meeting of the Mapai Secretariat on the issue of alignment with Achdut Avodah.

Eighteen members of the Secretariat voted for the Prime Minister's proposal, which stated that negotiations to the present time formed a basis for alignment be-

Golda Meir, Abba Eban and Other Top Leaders Support Levi's Proposal

Minister Moshe Dayan reportedly took no part in the voting though he attended the meeting which lasted from 6:30 Monday evening to 2:30 Tuesday morning.

Joseph Almogi, Development Minister Moshe Dayan reportedly

Abba Eban and Tel Aviv Mayor Mordechai Namir, Jewish Agency Executive Chairman Moshe Sharett and Mrs. Meir sent their supporting votes in writing.

Warns Lavon Followers

In ending the debate, Premier Eshkol said he hoped that Lavon's followers would not break with the party. If they did, he added, and joined Achdut Avodah, there

A Statement of Aims and Principles

WE DEEM IT APPROPRIATE, in this our inaugural issue, to state the aims and principles which have motivated us in establishing this new publication, the Cleveland Jewish News. The Jewish News is published by the Cleveland Jewish Publication Company, a non-profit corporation. Our aims are:

To provide the Jewish community of Greater Cleveland with a quality weekly newspaper which will fully present local, national, and world news of Jewish interest.

To offer commentary, interpretation, and authentic background on events of the day, as a means of stimulating the concern and response vital to the fulfillment of our responsibilities as Americans and as Jews.

To enrich the cultural life both of individuals and the community through the presentation of features, articles, reviews, and other material of Jewish content and interest.

To provide a forum for comment by members of the community wishing to express their viewpoints on matters of Jewish interest.

The Cleveland Jewish News is not affiliated with any one program, organization, movement, or point of view within Jewish life, but expects to give expression to all phases of that life.

The News is completely independent: it is committed to the progress and significant survival of Jewish life and to the democratic traditions which have made our country a blessed land.

By the 1960s, both Anglo-Jewish weeklies had declined in their news reporting and in circulation. After careful study, a group of Jewish leaders chartered The Cleveland Jewish Publication Company and purchased the assets of the two newspapers. The first issue of *The Cleveland Jewish News* appeared October 30, 1964. (Cleveland *Jewish News*)

. . . it was only north of Superior Avenue
[along 105th Street] that the Jewish neighborhood really came into its own. Almost
every block from Superior to St. Clair had its
own *shul* and its own kosher meat market
—and fruit and vegetable markets, drug
stores, creameries, bakeries, and grocery
stores abounded. All of them were meeting
places where Jewish events were discussed
and where the shape of the day and the week
was permeated with the rhythm of Jewish
life, reflected not only in the almost total
closing down of business on the Jewish holidays, but also in the shared experiences of
shopping and dating and discussing in an
atmosphere that took Jewish concerns and
Yiddishkeit for granted. At class reunions
nostalgic memories are still traded—of
waiting for "my next" on Saturday night at
the jammed meat market, or buying corned
beef at Solomon's on Massie Avenue, or
smelling the newly baked rye and pumpernickel in any of the bakeries clustered around
Earle and Gooding Avenues.

from Merging Traditions

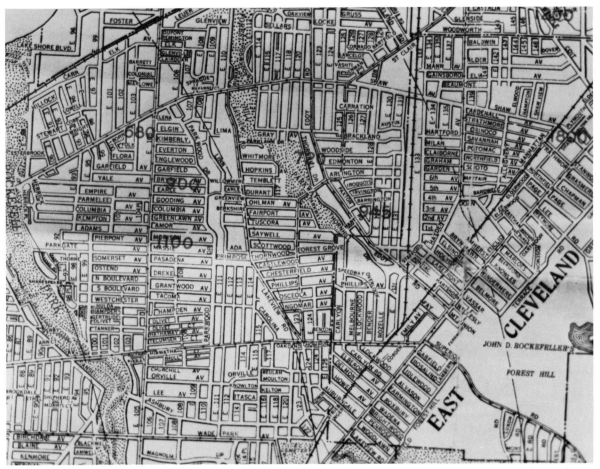

Map of the Glenville area in the heyday of Jewish residence. The area extended east of East Boulevard to the boundary with East Cleveland, and south from St. Clair Avenue to Wade Park Avenue. Its north-south streets were East 105th, Lakeview and East 123rd, each a main line for residents on the adjacent side streets. 1929 (Cleveland Directory)

Euclid Avenue at E. 105th was the gateway into the Glenville area. A flourishing business district, its restaurants, theaters and halls made it a center of night life, especially on weekends. The Alhambra Theater marquee dominates the photograph looking west down Euclid Avenue. ca. 1925 (Cleveland *Plain Dealer* Photo)

During the war years, the Federation of Jewish Charities and the Community Chest combined their fund-raising efforts in a single War Chest Appeal. This float of the Jewish Infant Orphan Home was photographed passing the Elysium, the ice-skating rink at E. 107th Street and Euclid Avenue, then used for military training. 1919 (Western Reserve Historical Society)

The Old ——— 10412 Euclid Ave. ——— Cleveland, Ohio

Weinberger's Drug, open 24 hours a day, on the southwest corner of the Euclid-E. 105th Street intersection, demonstrated Adolph Weinberger's progress in the quarter century since he opened his first pharmacy. ca. 1940 (Gray Drug Company)

1. Two major religious institutions adjoined Glenville. One was the Euclid Avenue Temple, 8206 Euclid Avenue, built by Congregation Anshe Chesed and dedicated in 1912. It was designed by the local firm of Israel J. Lehman and Theodore Schmidt. The education wing, added later, was the work of architect Joseph L. Weinberg. The congregation worshipped here until 1954, when it moved to the suburbs. It is now occupied by the Liberty Hill Baptist Church. 1916 (Cleveland *Plain Dealer* Photo)

2. A striking photograph of the ark in the main sanctuary by Geoffrey Landesman. 1943 (Western Reserve Historical Society)

3. A feature of the Euclid Avenue Temple was its imaginative use of brick in its external symbolism as seen in the tablets of the Ten Commandments above the main entrance to the Sanctuary. 1975 (Richard E. Karberg)

Rabbi Barnett R. Brickner was called to lead Congregation Anshe Chesed in 1925 and became a distinguished community leader during his 33 years of service. His debate with Clarence Darrow of Scopes trial fame in 1928 on the subject, "Is Man a Machine?," gained wide public attention. Rabbi Brickner was noted for his Sunday radio talks and received the Medal of Merit for his chaplaincy service during World War II. 1928 (Mrs. Rebecca Brickner)

1.

2.

3.

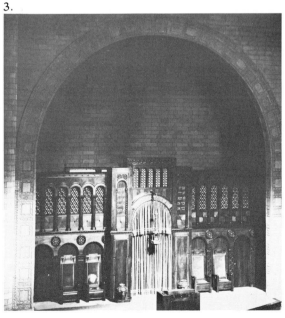

1.   Rabbi Abba Hillel Silver became leader of the Tifereth Israel Congregation in 1917. Soon thereafter, the congregation began to plan its new home at E. 105th and Ansel Road (Silver Park). Now a Cleveland landmark, The Temple was designed by Boston architect Charles R. Greco and dedicated in 1924. The photograph shows the dome over the sanctuary under construction. 1923 (The Temple)

2.   Built on an elevated wedge-shaped site, The Temple is in the Byzantine style, and its tile domes are a striking part of the University Circle area skyline. n.d. (The Temple)

3.   The richly designed ark beneath the vaulted dome of The Temple's main sanctuary. 1975 (Richard E. Karberg)

Rabbi Abba Hillel Silver is shown here with Mrs. Silver, at his left, at ground-breaking ceremonies for The Temple at Ansel Road and E. 105th Street (now University Circle at Silver Park). 1923 (American Jewish Archives, Cincinnati)

Rabbi Silver was a noted orator, and his Sunday morning sermons attracted large audiences including many of other faiths. "Silence is golden, but speech is Silver" was a popular saying among his appreciative listeners, shown here leaving The Temple. 1958 (American Jewish Archives, Cincinnati)

The automobile became the vehicle of social life soon after the turn of the century. Here Mollie Stearn takes a friend for a summer spin in the family auto, pausing for a moment in the driveway of the Abraham Stearn residence on Magnolia Drive. ca. 1908 (Mrs. Alan S. Geismer)

Older families began to leave the Woodland area long before Glenville acquired its status as a Jewish neighborhood. These families found new homes in the more fashionable Wade Park development within Glenville's orbit but outside its actual boundaries. Architect Frank B. Meade designed Emil Joseph's home at 1679 E. 115 Street in 1915. The study, filled with books and prints, is shown in the photograph. ca. 1922 (Frank E. Joseph)

1.

2.

1.   Jewish society in Cleveland frequently danced to the music of Samuel Rosenthal's orchestras. As impresario, Rosenthal provided both dance hall and orchestra as advertised in his brochure for the 1913–14 season. (Mrs. Walton L. Strauss)

2.   Jewish popular orchestra leaders began to make their mark on the Cleveland entertainment scene in the 1920s. Phil Spitalny (1890–1970), perhaps the best known of the musical Spitalny brothers, came to Cleveland in 1906 from Russia. From 1920 to 1927 his orchestra's soothing music was featured at the Allen Theater. After 1934, he gained national popularity with his all-girl orchestra, headlining "Evelyn and her Magic Violin" on tour and on radio's "Hour of Charm." He was also a composer of many sentimental, romantic songs. 1927 (Western Reserve Historical Society)

The chorus line and pit orchestra are shown during the performance of a Chassidic sketch at the Duchess Theater at E. 55th and Euclid Avenue. It was the major home of Yiddish theater in Cleveland, as movies and American culture patterns cut into its audience. 1923. (Mrs. Bertha Cutler)

1.

2.

1. Excelsior members held a sentimental farewell dinner before moving over to the Oakwood Country Club, which had been organized in 1907. 1931 (Western Reserve Historical Society)

2. Despite opposition, the Excelsior Club built its clubhouse and became a neighbor of Western Reserve University in 1909. Twenty-two years later when Excelsior merged with the Oakwood Country Club, the university purchased the building for use as a library and more recently as a student union. 1910 (*Jewish Review and Observer*)

Mt. Sinai Hospital at 1800 E. 100th Street was the first service institution to relocate in the Glenville area. The hospital was dedicated in 1916. ca. 1920. (Mt. Sinai Hospital)

A scene in the dispensary waiting room at the new Mt. Sinai Hospital. ca. 1917 (Mt. Sinai Hospital)

The second major service institution to move into the Glenville area was the Jewish Orthodox Home for the Aged, 736 Lakeview Road. It was built in 1921 and subsequently enlarged by several additions. 1956 (Menorah Park)

1.

2.

1. The Orthodox character of the Home is captured in this photograph of a Torah study group printed in J.O.H.A.'s golden anniversary brochure. 1956 (Menorah Park)

2. Community agencies usually follow after their clients. When Jewish families moved into the Arlington-E. 123rd Street district in sufficient numbers, the Council Educational Alliance opened its Arlington House branch about 1938 to extend its program beyond its base at the Cleveland Jewish Center. 1975 (Richard E. Karberg)

The Orthodox Jewish community preferred a compatible religious setting for its aged and its orphan children. Rather than see the children placed in the Jewish Orphan Home, the Orthodox gathered resources to establish the Orthodox Jewish Children's Home in 1919. Its Board of Directors included leading members of the Orthodox community. 1927 (Philip Greenberg)

1.

2.

1. The Cleveland Jewish Center at Grantwood Avenue and E. 105th Street stood imposingly in the heart of the Glenville community. Designed by A. F. Janowitz for Congregation Anshe Emeth, it was dedicated in 1920. The Center enriched Jewish life in the area for a generation as a social, educational, and recreational institution. The Cory United Methodist Church now occupies the building. ca. 1925 (Park Synagogue)

2. The cornice above main entrance to the Center's sanctuary bears the words from Psalms 29:2, "Ascribe unto the Lord the glory due unto his name; worship the Lord in the beauty of His holiness." 1974 (Richard E. Karberg)

2.

1. Orthodox synagogues are the common landmark of any densely settled Jewish neighborhood. Seventeen can be counted in the 1935 city directory, but there were undoubtedly others too small or indifferent to being listed. Except for Congregation Anshe Emeth (The Jewish Center) which turned to Conservative Judaism, all other congregations in the Glenville area were Orthodox. Congregation Oheb Zedek (Lovers of Righteousness), a long, two-story red brick structure at the corner of Morison Avenue and Parkwood Drive, was dedicated in 1922. Led for many years by Rabbi Israel Porath, it was an important center of Orthodox life. 1922 (Mrs. Louis Engelberg)

2. Congregation Beth Hamidrash Hagodol, known familiarly as the "Tacoma Shul," 1161 E. 105th Street, stood out because of its round columns. When the congregation moved in the 1950s, the building was acquired by the Greater Abyssinia Baptist Church. 1975 (Richard E. Karberg)

Driven from its home during the Nazi Holocaust, the renowned Yeshiva of Telshe, Lithuania, relocated in Cleveland in 1941, in a residence in the Glenville area. By 1947 with a growing student body drawn from many parts of the world, it moved to the Oak Pythian Temple building on E. 105th Street near St. Clair Avenue. Students are shown here enjoying a Talmudic lesson in the old *Beth Hamidrash* (House of Study). ca. 1950 (Telshe Yeshiva)

1.

2.

1. For the residents of Glenville, E. 105th was Main Street. Old world culture and American ways thrived in a close physical and personal environment, which time has covered with ethnic enchantment. Solomon's Delicatessen on the corner of Massie Avenue was a favorite eating spot, as indicated by its "Open All Night" sign. 1928 (Cleveland Public Library)

2. No business street in a Jewish neighborhood was without its string of butcher shops and poultry stores to provide kosher meat products. These shops, such as Kline's on E. 105th near Amor Avenue, contributed to the area's distinctiveness. 1947 (Cleveland Board of Zoning Appeals)

1.

2.

1. The physical features of E. 105th were already set in the 1920s with street blocks of small red brick stores and apartment buildings, interrupted at intervals by corner synagogues. J. Spector Bakery and Creamery, delivery wagon parked in front, was located at the corner of Englewood Avenue. Glenville High School was down the street at the corner of Parkwood Drive. 1925 (Fraser Realty Co.)

2. Mantel's furniture and appliance store, corner of Pasadena and E. 105th Street, earlier housed a branch of the Union Trust Co. ca. 1946 (Mantel & Goetz, Inc.)

1.

2.

3.

1. Sherwin's Bakery, 888 E. 105th Street (Earle Avenue). 1932 (Louis Sherwin)

2. Sometimes window displays in the neighborhood were more artistic. Bread was an art medium at Sherwin's Bakery. In this war-time window scene, bread soldiers flank a war bonds poster; the Yiddish reads "For a better tomorrow." 1943 (Louis Sherwin)

3. The appetizer, above all other neighborhood stores, retains a special aroma of the past. Jewish food tastes are visible through the display window of Emil Sand's store at E. 105th Street and Yale. 1941 (Edwin Sand)

1.

2.

1. Next to Harry L. Cohen's Pharmacy, at 961 E. 105th Street (Greenlawn Avenue) is a grocery outlet of the Great Atlantic and Pacific Tea Company chain, no different outwardly from the small proprietary competitors around it. ca. 1930 (Fraser Realty Company)

2. Part of Glenville was already developed when Jews began to move into the area before the first World War. This was particularly true of homes just off E. 105th Street, such as that of Mr. & Mrs. Michael Michalovsky at 10512 Massie Avenue. 1912 (Mrs. Leonard Climo)

The narrow, crowded store, stacked from floor to ceiling, is part of the Glenville image of yesterday. Charles Asadowsky, proprietor of a corner grocery, 814 E. 105th, typifies this small merchant world. ca. 1923 (Gertrude Baron)

The section of Glenville, east of E. 105th St., became popularly known as "Superior-Through," when the Superior streetcar, once terminating at the car barns at Lakeview Road, was extended "through" to St. Clair to the north—a strongly Jewish neighborhood. As elsewhere in Glenville, most of the buildings were functional and not very prepossessing. The corner of Fairport and E. 123rd Street. ca. 1946 (Cleveland Board of Zoning Appeals)

1.   The block between Tuscora and Saywell Avenues on E. 123rd Street. 1957 (Cleveland Board of Zoning Appeals)

2.   The corner grocery at 424 Eddy Road. 1940 (Cleveland Board of Zoning Appeals)

3.   The corner at Primrose Avenue and Lakeview Road. 1946 (Cleveland Board of Zoning Appeals)

Whether food or hardware, shoppers entered the same stuffed store interiors. Only the owner, Elias Mantel, and his experienced helpers could possibly know where all the items were to be found at East End Glass. 1917 (Jewish Community Federation)

NOW OPEN
Morison Ave. Russian Turkish Bath House
10606 Morison Ave.

Russian-Turkish Baths are a pleasure for young and old.
Fifty modern well furnished bedrooms. Fine meals served in
our modern dining room.

Open Every Day Except Friday Night to Saturday Night
MIKVAH for women open every day
8 A. M. to 12 P. M.
Russian-Turkish Baths for Women
on Wednesday
Experienced Attendants
PHONE EDDY 9166
Mgrs.—M. BAER and N. GORDON

1. Unlike the Orange Street bathhouse in the Woodland area, the Morison Avenue bathhouse provided steam baths, sleeping rooms and meals; it also doubled as a *mikvah* (ritual bath) for women. 1925 (*Jewish Independent*)

2. The circle of life to passersby was symbolized by this outdoor monument display at 822 E. 105th Street. It complemented three Jewish funeral homes in the immediate vicinity. 1947 (Cleveland Board of Zoning Appeals)

3. A small movie house, the Crown, near Kempton Avenue, was situated directly on E. 105th. Its red brick facade blended modestly with the surrounding street facade. Converted later to a market and then partially destroyed by fire, all that remains today is its name in the tile floor. 1975 (Richard E. Karberg)

The stretch of Superior Avenue from E. 97th to E. 123rd was the southern tangent of Glenville's Jewish community. If anything, it had more of a Jewish flavor than its parallel, St. Clair Avenue. Superior, at one time within two blocks of E. 105th, housed the Manhattan, the sometime home of Yiddish theater in the area, the Bureau of Jewish Education, and the newspaper offices of *Die Yiddishe Velt* (the *Jewish World*). The scene pictured is east along Superior across the intersection with E. 105th. 1946 (Cleveland Board of Zoning Appeals)

The intersection of E. 105th and St. Clair Avenue was a large business center, perhaps best remembered today for three popular cinemas, the Uptown, Savoy and Doan. The marquee of the latter can be seen through the web of overhead trolley wires. 1921 (Cleveland Trust Company)

Forest City Enterprises, a national business complex, start out with a man and a store. Before Leonard Ratner and his brothers moved into building supplies and real estate, he was the proprietor of a creamery near Ashbury Avenue at 1406 E. 105th Street. 1922 (Mrs. Harlan Sherman)

The exterior photograph of Julie's Master Market, on Wade Park Avenue, illustrates a step in the transition to the modern Pick-N-Pay supermarket chain and the virtual disappearance of the corner grocery. 1932 (Julie Kravitz)

Commercial Bookbinding, 2231–2251 W. 110th Street, was the basis for the future World Publishing Company, whose two staples became the Bible and the dictionary. Alfred Cahen, founder of the original business, is in the center of his group of employees. 1929 (Ben D. Zevin)

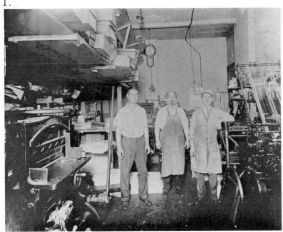

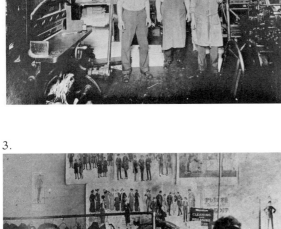

1. During this era, notices of sales, annual meetings, banquets, organization yearbooks and other printed materials were frequently in two languages, English and Yiddish. The Royal Printing Shop, 896 E. 105th Street, owned by Leo Moskowitz, offered this bilingual printing service. ca. 1926 (Mrs. Alex Estreicher)

2. Before there were refrigerators, there were icemen delivering ice to home customers, who signaled their needs by cards placed in their windows. Joe Friedman and Hymie Nadel pose with their ice truck on a Glenville side street. ca. 1925 (Mrs. Sanford Shore)

3. The neighborhood network of shops included many essential services. Each small section had its tailor to keep its residents well dressed, particularly for the holidays. Joseph Bernzweig is shown with his wife, Ricka, and infant son in his tailor shop located at Tuscora and E. 123rd Street. 1918 (Milton Berns)

1.

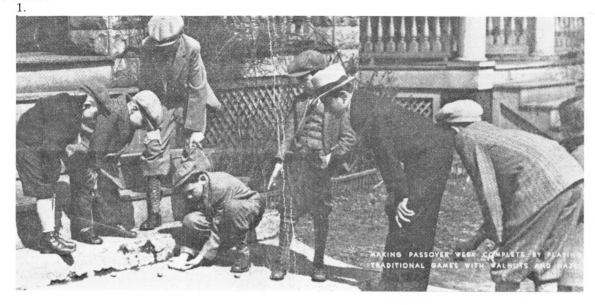

MAKING PASSOVER WEEK COMPLETE BY PLAYING
TRADITIONAL GAMES WITH WALNUTS AND NUTS

2.

1. A rare photograph of young people at play during Passover in the E. 105th Street area is copied from *Friday*, a monthly magazine which appeared for a short time in the mid-1930's. Its focus was on Cleveland Jewish life with articles contributed by young free-lance writers in the community. 1934 (Samuel L. Abrams)

2. Its people and their customs made E. 105th Street unique. One local newspaper photographed Mary Bloch shopping for Passover dishes on the avenue to alert its readers to the approach of the holiday. ca. 1930 (Sarah Bloch)

1. Pinochle and smoke shops were part of the Glenville home front as seen in this "Howdy, Neighbor" photograph in the local newspaper. 1940 (Cleveland *Press*)

2. The war years tied Glenville residents even closer together. Barney's restaurant-delicatessen on E. 105th was a social center for regulars who enjoyed its food and friendly atmosphere. 1940 (Cleveland *Press*)

3. Glenville Quality Food Store at 10128 St. Clair Avenue, operated by Leo and Louis Grossman (behind the counter), foreshadowed the changes in size and in food merchandising from the smaller crowded groceries, which were still very much part of the neighborhood scene. ca. 1912 (Fred Grossman)

American Greetings Corporation traces its origins back to Glenville. Jacob Sapirstein, the founder, started his business in a garage. At one time, the company was located on Superior near E. 123rd. How the business began is depicted in this painting showing the father and his three sons, who now direct this giant greeting card concern. n.d. (Irving Stone)

Clothing manufacture continued to be an important part of Cleveland's economy into the 1930s. Printz-Biederman, still operating in Cleveland, was established in 1894 and at one point employed over 300 workers. The scene is the sewing room. ca. 1930 (Cleveland Public Library)

In the early years, owners and employees worked together as a family in the clothing industry. Max Simon and David Simon (second row center), partners but not family related, started as tie manufacturers and built a successful men's wear operation. ca. 1925 (Miriam S. Klein)

1.

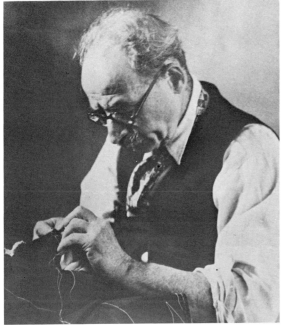

4.

3.

1.   Jews remained a prominent element in the garment industry's labor force. Simon Levy, who came to the United States after first emigrating to England from Lithuania, epitomizes their role in this sector of Cleveland's economic life. ca. 1930 (Benjamin B. Levy)

2.   Sub-contracting was a feature of the garment industry. All that was required were a few skilled workmen, some equipment and a workroom, preferably with some ventilation. Philip Nashkin's small company cut and sewed women's cloaks in a Prospect-E. 4th Street building until it was closed in the Depression. ca. 1925 (Mrs. David Guralnik)

3.   The manufacture of fur coats was a more specialized phase of the industry. The product was possibly more elegant than cloaks but not the shop conditions. Jacob Fishman and Jacob Matt operated their business in the C.A.C. building in downtown Cleveland. 1938 (Mrs. Mabel Snider)

4.   Cleveland-made dress goods were stocked by local department stores, such as the May Company. Welworth, a low-priced dress line, was introduced to the market in the 1920s by L. N. Gross Company, founded in 1898. 1926 (L. N. Gross Company)

1. The pharmaceutical profession had its share of Jewish practitioners. Milton and Yale Cohen, both pharmacists, owned drug stores in the Payne Avenue section. Milton is shown here at Yale Drug with a new product to sell after the repeal of prohibition. 1933 (Gray Drug Company)

2. With the automobile here to stay, Lester Blaushild secured a Chevrolet dealership in 1914 and started the oldest continuing auto firm in Cuyahoga County. 1914 (David Blaushild)

1.   Cleveland Jews owned businesses in all parts of the community. In the downtown area, Joseph Sachs operated a tobacco store and ice cream parlor in the Hotel Adams, where Higbee's Department Store now stands. ca. 1920 (Milton Sachs)

2.   Nathan Wolkov established his jewelry business on St. Clair Avenue in 1914. His brother, Sam, behind the counter, continued the business until 1969. 1920 (Evelyn Lewin)

3.   While Cleveland-made cigars continued to be hand-rolled by skilled Jewish workers, distributors progressed from horse-drawn delivery wagons to automobiles. The S.M. Mechalowitz Company, on Eagle Street, like the barbershop, was a male refuge. 1917 (Mrs. Belle Mechalowitz)

4.   A generation of children from socially conscious families were taught ballroom dancing and the social graces at the School of the Dance at E. 105th and Chester Avenue, established by Florence Shapero during the Depression. A class in party dress. ca. 1944 (Mrs. David Margolius)

1.

2.

3.

1. The names—Columbia, Parkwood, Chesterfield and Miles Standish elementary schools, and Empire and Patrick Henry junior high schools—evoke childhood memories for a generation who walked Glenville's streets to and from their studies. The second grade at Columbia posed for this class photo. 1921 (Gertrude Baron)

2. Glenville High School, 810 Parkwood Drive, gained an outstanding reputation for scholarship during the period from 1920-1950. Although the school no longer stands, it created a confraternity of graduates who attend class reunions in large numbers and keep its memory alive. ca. 1935 (Cleveland *Press*)

3. "Glenville will shine tonight" was a line in a school song. Many of its students did exactly that, not in sports but most often in extra-curricular activities in the arts and sciences, such as the debating team of 1923. (Irving Kane)

National Champions 1931 — Glenville High School Orchestra — Severance Hall Cleveland, O.

2.

1. Excellence in music added to Glenville High's reputation. The orchestra, directed by Ralph Rush, was acclaimed national scholastic champion in 1931. The orchestra sits proudly in first place on the stage of Severance Hall. (Herb Walker)

2. Occasionally and memorably a sports hero surfaced at Glenville. During the 1920s there were two: Saul Melziener, who became a football all-American at Carnegie Tech, and Benny Friedman (photo), who went on to the University of Michigan and was Walter Camp's all-American quarterback in 1926. He played professional football after graduation and was athletic director of Brandeis University from 1949-63. 1926. (Cleveland *Press*)

1.

2.

3.

1.   There were a few Jewish professional sports figures during the Glenville years. Jonah Goldman probably was the Cleveland Indians' first Jewish ball player. An infielder for the team in 1928, 1930 and 1931, his batting average was .224 in the era of Babe Ruth. 1930 (Cleveland *Press*)

2.   Jackie Davis, welterweight, was publicized as the "Jewish Angel," with a Star of David on his trunks. He engaged in 125 professional bouts between 1930-35 before retiring and becoming a referee. ca. 1932 (Mrs. Jack Davis)

3.   Alfred A. Benesch, shown here with his wife Helen, began his notable career of public service as public safety director under Mayor Newton D. Baker. He also held the unique distinction of serving continuously on the Cleveland Board of Education for 37 years from 1925-1962. 1915 (Mrs. George H. Rose)

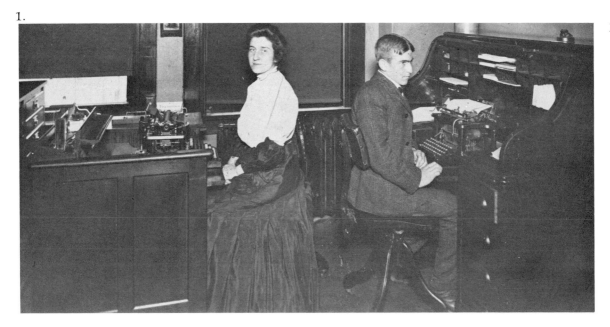

2.

1. The community's early synagogues were not the work of Jewish architects. The first Jewish architect to be identified in the community in the late 19th century was Israel Lehman. Next came Joseph Weinberg shown here in an office scene. He grew up in the Jewish Orphan Home and received his professional education at Harvard University. ca. 1915 (Mrs. Edith Weinberg)

2. Under the inspiring leadership of A. H. Friedland (seated fourth from left), renowned educator and Hebrew poet, his corps of dedicated teachers was the stimulus for a golden era of Hebrew learning in the 1920s and 1930s. Friedland, (*Chet Aleph*), was director of the Bureau of Jewish Education from 1924 until his death in 1939. ca. 1922 (Dr. Marvin Warshay)

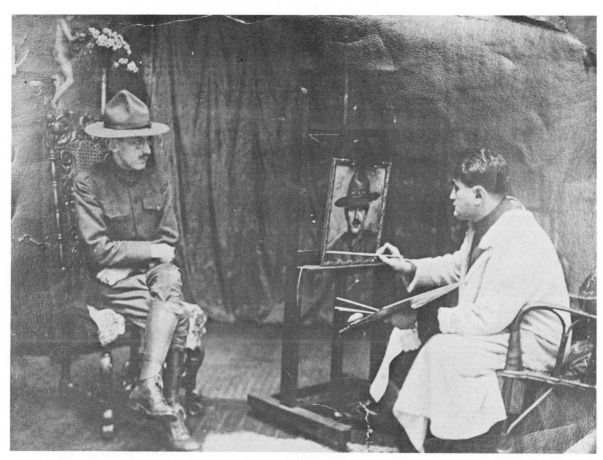

After the turn of the century, three local Jewish artists, sculptors William Zorach and Max Kalish and painter Abel "Buck" Warshawsky, began their climb to recognition and success. Warshawsky went to France to study art and served as a volunteer in the French Red Cross during World War I. Whenever his duties permitted, he returned to his studio to paint. 1918 (David Warshawsky)

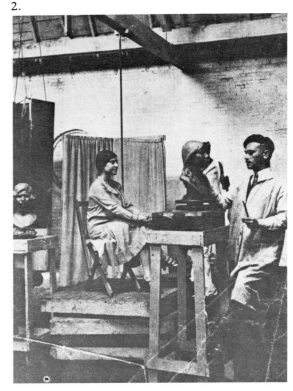

1.   William Zorach (1887–1966), the noted sculptor, spent his teen-age years in Cleveland before leaving home to continue his studies in New York and Paris. This early self-portrait was sketched in 1920. (Rosemary Lewis)

2.   Max Kalish's bronze statue of Abraham Lincoln in front of the Cleveland Board of Education, dedicated in 1932, is familiar to thousands of Clevelanders. A local newspaper photograph shows him in his Euclid Avenue studio sculpting a head of his wife, Alice. ca. 1933 (Donald M. Kalish)

1.

2.

3.

1. Musicians of Jewish background began to enrich Cleveland's cultural life at the turn of the century. Sol Marcosson (1860-1940) first came to Cleveland about 1897 as a violin soloist. He remained to gain acclaim as a member of the Cleveland Philharmonic Quartet and as concertmaster of the Cleveland Orchestra in 1918. In this photograph of the Quartet, he is seated at left with Charles Rychlik, James Johnson and Charles Heydler. ca. 1915 (F. Karl Grossman, *A History of Music in Cleveland*; Case Western Reserve University, 1972)

2. The Cleveland Institute of Music was established in 1920. Ernest Bloch (1890-1959), the noted composer who made extensive use of Jewish themes (*Trois Poèmes Juifs, Schelomo, Avodath Hakodesh*) was then a recent arrival in the United States. He became the Institute's first director, which he headed until 1925. 1920 (Cleveland Public Library)

3. Nikolai Sokoloff served as a conductor of the Cleveland Orchestra in its formative years 1918-1933. ca. 1920 (Western Reserve Historical Society)

1. The Jewish Singing Society, *Der Yiddisher Gesangs Farayn*, was organized in 1897 by Cantor Jacob Friedman of the Ohavei Emuna Anshe Russia congregation on Hill Street. Under the direction of Joseph Frank Nowodworski (seated center), it became an outstanding male chorus. Charles de Harrack was its director 1921-29. He was succeeded by Charles D. Dawe, who added women to the Society. ca. 1915 (Mrs. Charles de Harrack)

2. America's first Nobel Prize winner in 1907 was physicist Albert A. Michelson (1852-1931), son of Polish Jewish immigrants, who taught at Case School of Applied Science from 1882-1889. During these years, together with Edward W. Morley of Western Reserve University, he conducted the ether-drift experiments measuring the speed of light, which paved the way for Einstein's theory of relativity. He is shown here (at left) with two other Nobel winners, Albert Einstein and Robert A. Millikan, at a conference at the California Institute of Technology. 1931 (From a New York University brochure, *Hall of Fame for Great Americans*, 1973)

3. Established in 1894 the Cleveland Section of the National Council of Jewish Women - Rabbi Moses J. Gries, president—was from the outset an outstanding volunteer service organization. It was a model for other women's groups with different goals, such as Pioneer Women, Hadassah, Mizrachi Women and, more recently, Women's ORT. Shown here is a C.J.W. planning committee meeting. ca. 1925 (Western Reserve Historical Society)

1.

2.

3.

4.

1.   Maurice Maschke (1870-1936) was a prominent Republican political leader for over three decades. From his power base as chairman of the Cuyahoga County Republican Party, he was a key figure in the nomination and election of President Warren G. Harding. ca. 1925 (Western Reserve Historical Society)

2.   Judge Samuel H. Silbert was first elected judge of the Municipal Court of Cleveland in 1915. In 1922, he gained a place on the Common Pleas Court of Cuyahoga County and became its chief justice in 1953. In all, he served as judge for more than 50 years. ca. 1925 (Western Reserve Historical Society)

3.   Jewish participation in government was limited during the nineteenth century. The few who were active during the Woodland era were followed later by many others as they acquired professional training, particularly in the law. Edward J. Schweid, shown being sworn in as traction commission in Mayor Harold H. Burton's cabinet, carried out a major reorganization of Cleveland's transit system. 1935 (Mrs. Harold Friedman)

4.   Judge Mary B. Grossman, one of the first women jurists, was elected to Cleveland's Municipal Court in 1923 and was a judge until she retired in 1960. ca. 1925 (Western Reserve Historical Society)

1.

2.

3.

1. East European Jews as followers of Theodor Herzl made up the popular base for political Zionism. Cleveland was the site of national and regional Zionist conventions, the most notable being the 1921 American Zionist Conference at which Chaim Weizmann and Louis D. Brandeis split over the issue of resettlement of Palestine. The first annual convention of the Ohio Zionist Conference was held in Cleveland in 1932. (Erwin Blonder)

2. Zionist groups often added a social layer to their organizational objectives. Cleveland Hadassah, chartered in 1913, and the Pioneer Women's organization were early local women's groups with a Zionist focus. The Pioneer ladies of Chapter One pose for a group photo on a summer afternoon. 1938 (Mrs. F. Kitner)

3. A chain of sixteen gardens, thirteen of them established by nationality groups, stretches along East Boulevard from Superior to St. Clair in an outdoor display of Cleveland's ethnic diversity. The Hebrew Cultural Garden, second in the chain, was dedicated in 1926 and completed in 1937. Chaim Weizmann, later the first president of Israel, helped dedicate the garden, with Rabbi Abba Hillel Silver and City Manager William R. Hopkins participating. May 5, 1926 (Bureau of Jewish Education)

At the center of the garden, set in a pool, is a marble fountain with columns representing the seven pillars of wisdom. 1954 (Clara Lederer, *Their Paths Are Peace*)

. . . it was an era of innocence, good clean fun and unsophistication, when people lived together in amazing harmony and the strongest power was "mama-power."

Friendships that flourished in that great old neighborhood, that stretched from East 119th and Kinsman to 154th and from Bartlett to Milverton, have endured to this day.

Council Educational Alliance, 13512 Kinsman, was the meeting grounds of many boys and girls, teen-age clubs in a blending of Jewish nourishment, creative and athletic activities, and social pursuits. . . .

The long streets were always filled with kids playing baseball . . . telephones had three party lines . . . and large front porches held gobs of kids every night sitting on the swing and on the railings to joke around, exchange ideas and neck—after the grown-ups disappeared.

Violet Spevack
Cleveland Jewish News
January 21, 1972

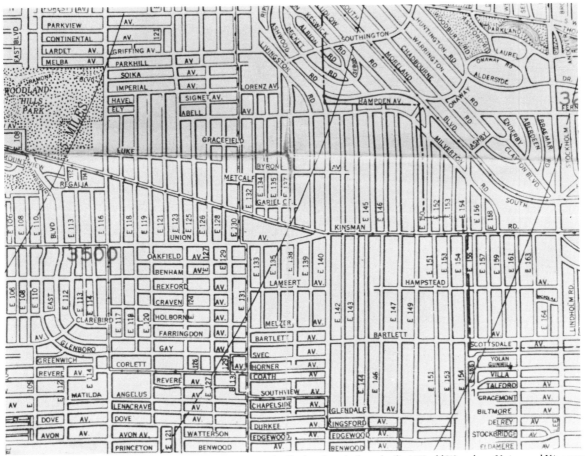

The Jewish section of the Mt. Pleasant-Kinsman area gradually developed after the first World War along Union and Kinsman Avenues, east of the Woodland Hills section. By the 1930s many Jewish families were to be found east of East 140th Street, where Union ended, between Milverton on the north and Bartlett on the south. 1929 (Cleveland *City Directory*)

1.

2.

1.   Like any neighborhood main street, Kinsman blocks were lined with convenience stores to serve residents—poultry and butcher shops, groceries, delicatessens. There were even occasional furniture and auto showrooms. This series of photographs captures the physical quality of the street. A dry goods store, 12701 Kinsman, owned by William F. Schwartz, one of the earliest Jewish proprietors in the area. 1918 (Dr. Edward D. Schwartz)

2.   Bennie Blaushild's Dodge-Plymouth showroom, 14309 Kinsman. 1935 (Mrs. Sanford Miller)

1. Rapaport Poultry, 12114 Kinsman. 1946 (Cleveland Board of Zoning Appeals)

2. The Press-Goldberg furniture store, 13800 Kinsman. 1950 (Cleveland Board of Zoning Appeals)

3. The street was also a front porch for families living above its shops; E. 152nd and Kinsman. 1948 (Cleveland Board of Zoning Appeals)

Goldie and Joseph Fishman's butcher shop, 14700 Kinsman. ca. 1929 (Mrs. Goldie Alper)

The corner delicatessen functioned as informal gathering place for friends to meet and plan an evening's social activities. Louis Katz's store at E. 147th and Kinsman was a favorite spot for young men in the vicinity. A rest room for a meal or occasional nap was behind the door at the rear. ca. 1929 (Mrs. Fannie Katz)

1.

MT. PLEASANT HOUSE

3.

2.

1.   An early focal point of community activity was the residence used as the Mt. Pleasant branch of the Council Educational Alliance at 3335 E. 118th Street. 1923 (*Jewish Independent*)

2.   Jewish learning for many Kinsman youngsters began at the "Talmud Torah," a branch of the Cleveland Hebrew Schools, located on the ground floor of a small apartment building at 13407 Kinsman during the years 1928-49. The sketch softens the drab lines of the structure. ca. 1928 (Cleveland Hebrew Schools)

3.   Jewish merchants owned small shops in many Cleveland neighborhoods after the turn of the century. In the Polish-Russian section adjacent to Mt. Pleasant, Hyman and Rose Pinhesic had the language skills to make buying at their grocery store, 7302 Union, easier for their customers. ca. 1919 (Hyman Pinhesic)

1.   Several neighborhood theaters dotted Kinsman Avenue. The marquee of the Imperial at E. 142nd Street was photographed in the days before television dimmed its lights. 1938 (Cleveland Zoning Board)

2.   Kinsman housing was typically two-family frame, four-suite apartment buildings or, on the main street, a combination of first-floor stores and second floor suites; single family homes were uncommon. The pattern contrasts with the more varied housing style found in the Glenville area. These apartments of red brick on E. 140th Street are outwardly unchanged since they were first built in the 1920s. 1975 (Richard E. Karberg)

3.   The Kinsman style in housing also reflects the speed with which the area was developed following the First World War. This row of two-family homes on E. 147th Street was duplicated by the hundreds in the area's many side streets. 1975 (Richard E. Karberg)

1.

1. Kinsman teen-agers came together for their last years of public schooling at John Adams High School, 3817 E. 116th Street, dedicated in 1923 as a junior high school and later designated a senior high school. At the right is the horse-drawn hot waffle wagon. ca. 1925 (Cleveland *Press*)

2. The interior of a dry goods store in an adjacent ethnic neighborhood, Hungarian, at 8915 Buckeye; proprietor Charles Katz. ca. 1932 (Iris Fishman)

1.

2.

1. Cleveland women began holding suffrage-peace rallies with the outbreak of World War I. Their dedication continued in the post-war years. On May 19, 1924, a contingent of women and children from the Mt. Pleasant branch of the Council Educational Alliance participated in a march for peace in downtown Cleveland. (Albert M. Brown)

2. Congregation Shomrei Hadas (Keepers of the Faith), 12302 Parkhill, was located in the mid-1920s on the edge of Mt. Pleasant. It survived until 1973 as a vestige of Jewish religious life in southeast Cleveland. Most of its remaining members joined the Taylor Road Synagogue, and its synagogue was sold to the Second Trinity Baptist Church. 1975 (Richard E. Karberg)

1.

2.

1. CEA offered a variety of activities. A music class provided youngsters with an opportunity for music making. ca. 1945 (*Jewish Independent*)

2. As the neighborhood grew and Jewish families moved further east, community services moved with them. The Council Educational Alliance, 13512 Kinsman Avenue, was opened in 1928 opposite the Carpenters Hall. The two buildings made that corner a pivot of Kinsman life in the 1930s. In the mid-1950s the branch was closed and the building sold. 1975 (Richard E. Karberg)

1. On Jewish holidays, CEA often turned its gymnasium into a festival hall. Here member families enjoy a Purim carnival. 1949 (*Jewish Independent*)

2. The CEA Triangles, a boys' club, feature outdoor sports in this swinging strike at Woodland Hills Park. 1921 (Leo M. Ascherman)

1.

2.

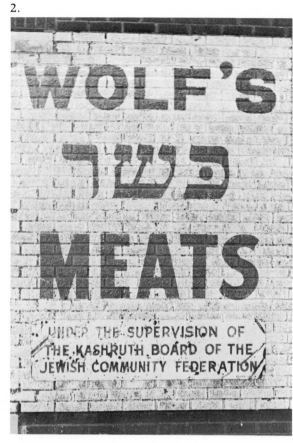

1.   For many Cleveland Jews World War I was their initial extensive experience with the military. A few served in the then more exotic flying corps. Stanley Kaplan sent this snapshot home from his Texas training base. 1918 (Ben Kaplan)

2.   Except for building cornerstones and religious symbols, only one sign, Wolf's Kosher Meat Market, continues to proclaim a Jewish presence in the Kinsman area. Organized in 1946, the Kashrut Board reestablished confidence among buyers of kosher meat products. At its peak the Board had 67 members; today, their number has declined to 13. 1975 (Richard E. Karberg)

BANQUET GIVEN IN HONOR
OF
RABBI ABBA HILLEL SILVER
BY THE JEWISH FARMERS OF GENEVA
SEPT. 3, 1928

2.

1. Some Jews preferred farming to city life. A small colony of Jewish farmers centered in the Geneva, Ohio, region assembled in 1928 for a banquet honoring Rabbi Abba Hillel Silver. (Jules Flock)

2. With the doors to mass immigration shut and Eastern Europe in the grip of political and economic upheaval, Jews in the Brest-Litovsk region received aid through the Cleveland Brisker Relief Committee. 1927 (Ida Schwartz)

1.

2.

3.

1.　An immigrant generation held many memories and ties to the "old country." Elderly parents and grandparents sometimes preferred to stay behind, and often hard choices had to be made, leading at times to permanent separation. In this photograph, Shmuel Ruthstein stands alongside the tombstone of his son in Swienciany, Lithuania. The Yiddish caption at the base reads: "Provided by his wife and children in America." ca. 1925 (Mrs. Sam Kasimov)

2.　Houses of worship were an integral part of institutional life in the Mt. Pleasant section. Congregation Niveh Zedek (Dwelling Place of Justice), 11901 Union Avenue, began holding services in the area by 1920 and erected its synagogue later in the decade. When the congregation left the area, it became part of the Warrensville Center Synagogue; its house of prayer is now the Second Tabernacle Baptist Church. 1975 (Richard E. Karberg)

3.　Temple Beth El (House of God) at 15808 Chagrin Boulevard is located in Shaker Heights on the eastern rim of the Kinsman section. Of the seven Orthodox Jewish houses of worship in the area in 1954, when Beth El was erected, today only it remains. 1975　(Richard E. Karberg)

1.

2.

3.

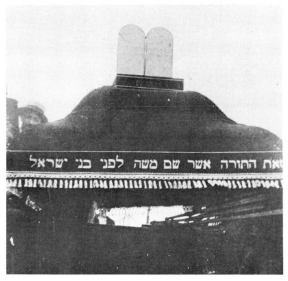

1. The Kinsman Jewish Center, 14623 Kinsman Avenue, was the home of the Orthodox B'nai Jacob Kol Israel (Sons of Jacob All Israel) Congregation, but it was not the complete neighborhood center its name suggests. The building now houses the Warren Bible Institute. 1975 (Richard E. Karberg)

2. Synagogue life in Mt. Pleasant-Kinsman was completely Orthodox. No Conservative or Reform congregations were established in the area. About 1922 the home of Reb Shmiel Levine, 3448 East 149th Street, became the temporary location of Ohel Yavne (Tent of Yavne) congregation. Reb Levine was its spiritual leader, but he earned his livelihood during the week as a floor scraper. ca. 1925 (Ben Levine)

3. Later, when Ohel Yavne built its synagogue, Reb Levine constructed an elaborate *chupah* (canopy) for transfer of the Torah to the new ark. The *chupah* was also used later for outdoor wedding ceremonies. ca. 1925 (Ben Levine)

Members of Ohel Yavne are shown here carrying the Torah scrolls under the *chupah* into the living room-sanctuary of the Levine home. ca. 1922 (Ben Levine)

The older members needed to rest after the Torah procession. Two young musicians apparently provided the music for the joyous walk. ca. 1922 (Ben Levine)

1.

2.

3.

1. Jewish labor helped give Mt. Pleasant-Kinsman its unique character. The square, brick Jewish Carpenters Hall at 135th Street and Kinsman was the focus of union business and social activity in the 1930s. Members of the Jewish Painters Union pose at the rear of the building with their business agent. ca. 1932 (Jewish Community Federation)

2. The Workmen's Center was the main branch of the *Arbeiter Ring*, a Jewish workers' organization with a socialist orientation. Erected in 1927 at 3471 E. 147th Street, the Center helped add to Kinsman's distinctiveness as a working class area. It is now occupied by Jehovah's Witnesses. 1975 (Richard E. Karberg)

3. The *Arbeiter Ring* (Workmen's Circle) stressed Yiddish as the language of its members. By contrast social and fraternal organizations in the mid-19th Century enforced rules requiring English be spoken at meetings as a language learning technique. Shown here are members of the Executive Committee. ca. 1928 (Mrs. Irwin Beckenstein)

The Workmen's Circle Band evolved in part from the Cleveland Jewish Band. I. J. Masten, head of the Musicians Union, was also a carry-over as director of both groups. It was primarily a concert band with a semi-popular and classical repertoire. ca. 1924 (Irving Markowitz)

The last local Jewish survivor of the Civil War, Herman Stern, is photographed with Jewish veterans of later wars. Stern, wearing his campaign hat, fought with a Pennsylvania regiment; he is seated third row center. 1921 (Theodore S. Koplik)

Memories of Kinsman for the older generation include echoes of the Kinsman streetcar line, which ran from E. 159th Street to E. 4th and Prospect. This model appeared on the avenue after 1945. (Cleveland Public Library)

There were two principal sources for the photographs in this book. Some were taken especially for the Jewish Community Federation and its agencies, and for the most part deal with Jewish life today and of the recent past. These photographs are important, but they obviously cannot have the historic value and nostalgic appeal of many of the older views which appear in this volume.

The gathering, researching and duplication of these older photographs constitute their own story. The older photographs were copied from original prints and negatives that came from a variety of sources. In some instances, newsprint photos were copied, despite technical limitations, because of their historic importance. Publicity, newspaper articles and even a photo contest broadened the search. Institutions, private and public archives, and commercial firms were asked for old photographs that might be useful in this work. The word "asked" is really inadequate to describe what happened, because in the three year period during which photographs were assembled, the first question the researchers put to almost anyone they met was, "Do you have any old photographs?" The job of gathering these photographs sometimes took the form of polite badgering; at other times it constituted a typical detective story, as each lead was methodically followed on the trail of another cache of photographs.

At times the photo seekers took to the field and poked through dusty boxes stored in attics or dingy basements. At other times they pored over long-unopened file cases and Holinger archival boxes. These pursuits often yielded photographs which gratified the researchers and brought to life many fragmentary records whose truths have become part of community legend.

As the photographs were collected, they were copied onto 35 or 120 mm. roll film with either Plus X or Panatomic X film. Over two thousand photographs were assembled in this way, not only for display but to insure preservation of this graphic past. Most of the original photographs were returned to the lenders, although some were placed, with their lenders' consent, in the photo files of the Cleveland Jewish Archives of The Western Reserve Historical Society.

Enlargements of 8 by 10 inches were made from the negatives of photographs selected for exhibit or publication. Sometimes the prints made in this manner were of very good quality, indistinguishable from negatives exposed today. In fact, the work of professional street photographers in the decades at the turn of the century made copying easy. Unfortunately, in other instances, the photographs were faded, dark, out of focus or damaged by poor preservation or inadequate care in making the originals. In most cases, it was decided to leave the prints as they were. Some prints—when it could be done without interfering with the integrity of the original photography—were sent to a retoucher who performed minor miracles in

making the photograph clearer. It is hoped
that the reader, upon viewing what is obviously a poor photograph, will understand
that it was the intention to present the original
image in order to enhance its reality for today.

These photographs, which were taken at the
time without thought to publication, present
an invaluable way of looking at the history
of a community group. The images remain,
unchanged for all time, as documentary evidence of people, places and traditions in
a rapidly changing world.

Richard E. Karberg
Photographer

This book was composed by The Oberlin Printing Company, Elyria, Ohio; set in Palatino type and printed on Michigan Matte paper. It was bound in Holliston Roxite by John Dekker & Son, Grand Rapids, Michigan.

Designed by Gary Gore.